040353

ADOPTED?

ADOPTED?
A Canadian guide for adopted adults in search of their origins

Clare Marcus

International Self-Counsel Press Ltd.
Head and Editorial Office
Vancouver
Toronto   Seattle

Canadian Cataloguing in Publication Data

Marcus, Clare, 1924-
    Adopted?

    (Self-Counsel series)
    Bibliography: p.
    ISBN 0-88908-050-X

    1. Adoption - Canada.   2. Genealogy.

    I. Title.   II. Series
    HV875.M37   362.7′34   C79-091054-3

International Self-Counsel Press Ltd.
Head and Editorial Office
306 West 25th Street
North Vancouver, British Columbia V7N 2G1
Telephone: (604) 986-3366
Toronto   Vancouver   Seattle

CONTENTS

APPENDIXES

LIST OF SAMPLES

The self-perception of all of us is partly based on what our parents and ancestors have been, going back many generations. Adoptees, too, wish to base themselves not only on their adoptive parents, but also on what their original parents and forebears have been, going back many generations. It is the writer's view, based on his findings, that no person should be cut off from his origins.

— John Triseliotis,
In Search of Origins,
The Experiences of
Adopted People (London: Routledge & Kegan Paul Ltd., 1973).

PREFACE

This book is meant to serve as a road map for adopted adults seeking to find their origins.

A search for origins takes place in a bewildering territory where many avenues still remain closed; the book will suggest some routes to help you to your destination. It will help you get started and suggest resources where you may obtain further assistance.

It might be best to read the book through completely first to gain a perspective, then go back to the step-by-step suggestions. Whether you were born in Canada or in some other country, the process is much the same.

When you have completed your search and prepared your own family history, you will not only have traced your origins but will know yourself better. You will have grown, and you will know what you wanted to know all along.

ACKNOWLEDGMENTS

The author gratefully acknowledges the generous assistance of adoptee groups, adoptive parents, birth parents, various other individuals, provincial and state government staff, and a supporting family.

1

WHY YOU NEED TO KNOW

Now that genealogy has become the most popular avocation in North America, it is not surprising that adopted adults are among those interested in tracing their origins.

For the adopted person biological roots form the missing first chapter of the book of life.

It is only in recent years that adopted adults have felt free to insist on their right to know their complete identity. Not too long ago an adoptee who asked questions about origins was likely to be considered maladjusted. Today, more and more people recognize the validity of this deep need to know. Knowing where we came from helps us to understand who we are today.

The hard work and emotional investment of a search for your origins can't logically be dismissed as casual curiosity. There are many sound reasons for needing to know, reasons that override the original parents' right to confidentiality. This is information that only they can provide. *It is the one thing they can do for their offspring even if they do not wish to have any personal contact.*

A way can be found to transmit information. In fact, so much information is continually transmitted about all of us, often without our knowledge, that no one has complete confidentiality.

Massive link-ups with computer information systems provide instant data feeding of the most personal, financial and medical information on anyone to almost anyone. Telephones are tapped, police can open personal mail, yet, quaintly, old notions of confidentiality persist in keeping from adopted people the kind of basic information required to make decisions on important matters in life. One has to question whose best interests are receiving priority.

The search often begins with the death of adoptive parents, the adopted person's marriage, or some other deeply personal and important life event. The birth of a child frequently is the trigger for active search, for giving birth is so moving an experience that women say they could not help but wonder then about their first mother, finding it impossible to believe that their own birth could have been forgotten.

My mother certainly never forgot my birth or the date. "It was a sad day for me when I had to leave you behind," she was to tell me recently. "They (people from the maternity home) put me on the train to make sure I would not go back for you."

For years, individual adopted people in Canada raised questions about their origins, but were reluctant to speak up because they were unaware that others had the same needs.

My own search, for example, began with questions in 1941 and continued, spasmodically, for 37 years. The final phase of this search was underway shortly after a group called Parent Finders was born. Hearing two of the founders on a radio program proved to be a turning point in my search. Suddenly I knew that others were doing the same thing. Others shared my needs and were not ashamed to admit it publicly. Somebody, at last, was willing to help me.

a. WHO DO I LOOK LIKE?

One of the common threads in searching, says Joan Vanstone, a founder of Parent Finders (see page 20), is the adoptee's need to find a relative of similar appearance. The natural child sees in his parents or relatives a "mirroring" of himself; for the adopted person that aid to self-identity is not there. "I felt that I had finally found my way home," she says of this experience in her own search.

Vanstone began her search in middle life and credits her adoptive mother with her desire to find biological roots. "She was orphaned herself at the age of 13 but she always talked about her family and instilled in me a sense of history," Vanstone says. When looking through photo albums kept by her adoptive mother, the thought came to her that people in those pictures "were my family, but they weren't my ancestors. I was conscious of that difference."

Although her natural parents had died long before she was able to trace them, Vanstone has found and met other members of her original family. "You start with zero and you add on from there. Even though my mother had died I was glad to have found her. I met a close friend of her's and I have pictures of my mother."

b. ETHNIC TRADITIONS

For my foster family, as for millions of people in North America, the traditions and language of original nationality were tremendously important. When I was a child, questions were not answered unless asked in Lettish and that language was mastered before English. My text for learning to read was a collection of old Latvian tales.

I was conscious of the importance of ethnic heritage, and of the need to know my own heritage, by the time I began my search.

When I finally learned that my ethnic background was Welsh and Flemmish and that I was born at Healthwin Hospital in Winnipeg, I was overwhelmed and excited. Elated, I sailed out of the government office, a new person who had been born to real people in a hospital just like everyone else and had been connected to definite national origins. What a sense of normalcy that information gave me!

c. MEDICAL HISTORY

Only another adoptee knows the feeling of disconnection that comes when a doctor asks about family medical history, as happens sooner or later. "Any diabetes in your family? Any heart trouble?" And always we must say, "I don't know." This lack of knowledge that most people take for granted is frustrating and demeaning.

Sometimes it can be more serious than frustrating. When there are serious medical problems, a lack of medical history in the family can result in grave consequences. In March 1978, Alan Daniel's story in the *Vancouver Sun* told of a 29-year-old diabetic mother of two young children who, in 1975, gave herself an overdose of insulin and died. The published story told how the woman had been afraid of the unknown, her fears based on a past to which she had no access.

"She was an adopted child," wrote Daniels (proving once again that adopted people are forever considered adopted children).

"Stricken with epilepsy and diabetes, all attempts to locate her natural parents and obtain details of their medical history ended in failure. She became depressed at the prospect of further hereditary medical problems — a depression which led to suicide."

Joan Vanstone of Parent Finders, who with a social worker had been trying to help the woman obtain the information she needed, said: "She was haunted by the unknown in her background. She had repeatedly asked for information through Children's Aid but couldn't find her birth name or any other identifiable background information on which she could begin a search."

This happened even though, like most adoption statutes, the Adoption Act of British Columbia provides for disclosure of sealed information on "good cause" shown to the satisfaction of the court.

The anonymity of the adoption procedure was devised before it was known that a great variety of medical risk factors known at birth give rise to preventable maladies. Furthermore, many medical conditions are hereditary and still more are suspected of being genetically transmitted. It would seem mandatory then to maintain complete family and birth history in adoption files, with further updating as necessary, to be available to adopting parents and adoptees when required.

The time when most adopted adults want to know about medical history is when they are contemplating marriage and the bearing of children. This is quite normal; why else are genetic counselling units established?

Not only do adopted adults have a secret fear of inadvertently marrying a blood relative through lack of knowledge about biological background, but there are also unknown genetic factors that could affect any children born to them. Other people are more likely to know the risks and can benefit from genetic counselling.

People who want the utmost secrecy in adoption matters tend to discount the risk of marrying a relative, but recently an adoptee in Kitchener, Ontario found her first mother and discovered she herself was married to her third cousin.

2

ACCESS TO ADOPTION RECORDS

a. WHAT IS ADOPTION?

Mythology, secrecy and fear surround the practice of adoption as it is known today. Children are placed with adopting parents "as if" born to that family, ties with natural parents and sometimes siblings are severed, and the process is wrapped tightly within a shroud of confidentiality designed to bury true origins forever.

The "as if" concept is spelled out in the Adoption Act of British Columbia in Section 10:

> (1) For all purposes an adopted child becomes upon adoption the child of the adopting parent, and the adopting parent becomes the parent of the child, as if the child had been born to that parent in lawful wedlock.
>
> (2) For all purposes an adopted child ceases upon adoption to be the child of his existing parents (whether his natural parents or. his adopting parents under a previous adoption), and the existing parents of the adopted child cease to be his parents.

The wording about adoption differs in the legislation of the various provinces, but the concept and effect are the same.

Adoption has not always been considered in this light and the "as if" concept is not etched in stone. Formal, legalized adoption has existed in Canada for about 50 years and until recently the method was not questioned, nor was research undertaken to assess how well it served all of the parties involved (commonly referred to as the adoption triangle).

1. Adoption in early history

There has always been a need for some form of surrogate parenting of orphaned or unwanted children since the earliest days of humans. The methods of providing this care have changed with time and will continue to change to meet recognized needs.

The late Jacob Bronowski, author of *The Ascent of Man*, maintained that the first socialization step taken within groups, tribes, or bands was the acceptance of collective responsibility for orphaned children. Skulls and skeletons of Australopithecus, a cousin of humans who lived two million years ago, show that most of them died before the age of 20. This suggested to Bronowski that there must have been many orphans and, consequently, a social organization for looking after them in the community. Primitive tribes used the idea of adoption to combine with one another, and some ancient civilizations practised adoption to assure the continuation of their ancestor worship customs.

Moses, the Biblical story tells us, was found in a basket among the reeds by the bank of the Nile by the Pharoah's daughter. She adopted him and gave him the name of Moses. But his natural mother suckled him and one day when Moses was grown up, according to the *New English Bible*, "he went out to his own kinsmen and saw them at their heavy labor."

Romulus and Remus, so the legend goes, were set adrift in a basket on the Tiber River. Fortunately, they drifted safely to shore where a she-wolf rescued and nurtured them. By and by, the royal shepherd Faustulus and his wife Acca Larentia found the babies and took them home to raise. When they were grown, the boys *learned their true identity*. They were the twin sons of the god Mars and Rhea Silvia, daughter of Numitor, king of Alba Longa, whose throne was usurped by his brother Amulius. The grown twins killed Amulius and restored Numitor to the throne, and established their own city on the Tiber. Thus, Romulus is said to be the true founder of Rome about 753 B.C.

The foundations of modern adoption practices were laid in the time of the Roman Empire when the father had complete authority over his children, and this extended to the adopted child. All ties with the biological family were cut and the contract was binding. This was not done to serve the child's interests, but so that the adoptee could continue the adopter's family and perpetuate the family's religious beliefs.

Infanticide, common in ancient societies as a means of disposing of unwanted children, continued into more recent times. "Originally, the unwed mother had no rights or services, and consequently concealed or even destroyed her offspring," wrote Benjamin Schlesinger, professor of social work at the University of Toronto.

2. Adoption practices in Canada

It was 1826 before the first legislation was passed in Upper Canada "to prevent the destroying and murdering of bastard children."

Between Confederation and World War I, 73 000 children were sent to Canada from Great Britain for distribution to Canadian families. The first group of 50 little girls from the Kirkdale Workhouse in Liverpool landed in Quebec in November 1869, and thousands of girls and boys followed.

These orphans and street urchins were gathered up and shipped off to a strange land, going first to distributing homes or local orphanages before being indentured or adopted. If they were under the age of nine, they could be adopted under a contract that allowed for return of the child who proved unsatisfactory, a situation that has not changed today, and older children generally were indentured as servants.

It is estimated that 2 000 000 Canadians can trace their ancestry to one of those homeless, often exploited, children, and some of the survivors are still trying to trace

8

their roots. One is a blind woman in her eighties, who never gave up hope of one day finding her family from whom she was separated when placed in an English orphanage at the age of four. She was shipped to Canada in 1905 and placed with a family in Ontario, a traumatic experience that left lifelong wounds, which she hopes to heal in her final years by tracing her roots.

Long before this lady arrived in Canada as a child, the need for improved child care practices was seen. The organization of children's aid societies in the late 19th and early 20th centuries hastened the end of street begging and peddling of small wares by hungry children, youthful immorality and truancy.

> . . . the Societies have rescued children from the control of criminals, drunkards and depraved women; have gathered up from the poorhouse, jails and refuges many unwanted and motherless little ones, and have transplanted upward of a thousand children from a condition of misery and destitution into homes of respectability and Christian culture.

That quote is from *Women of Canada, Their Life and Work*, compiled by the National Council of Women of Canada and published for distribution at the Paris International Exhibition in 1900.

John Joseph Kelso, Ontario's superintendent of neglected and dependent children, led in the movement for improved child care that began in the late 1800s. In 1891, **when the Children's Aid Society was formed in Toronto,** there were 41 orphanages in Canada holding 3 827 children. Orphaned and unwanted children continued to fill orphanages for many years until, in the 1940s it was deemed unhealthy for children to be raised in institutions.

People arranged their own adoptions prior to the adoption legislation enacted in Canadian provinces in the late 1920s, and they continued to advertise their unwanted children into the early 1930s. Nurses and doctors often acted as the brokers in these arrangements. Only desperation could account for some of the advertisements.

> Party who adopted little girl Maple Leaf Apts., Fort Rouge, July 1919 would like to communicate with her mother. Box . . . .

Had something gone wrong? Did they want to give her back? Or, had they belatedly decided to obtain a family history to pass on to the child in her maturity?

> Childless farm couple wants infant from birth for adoption, with dowry. Same will inherit. Box . . . .
>
> Manitoba Free Press, 1929
>
> Lovely baby girl four months old for adoption; brown hair and blue eyes. Box . . . .
>
> For adoption, baby girl ten days old. Protestant. Finest parents. Box . . . .
>
> Beautiful baby boy eight months old for adoption. Protestant and of English parents. Box . . . .
>
> Winnipeg Free Press, 1930

There have been at least 500 000 legal adoptions in Canada since the 1920s when adoption legislation came into being, according to Philip Hepworth, associate professor at the University of Regina, and former program director for the Canadian Council on Social Development.

Those are the known adoptions. It is possible that as many more privately arranged, native custom adoptions, and informal "accepted-into-the-family" adoptions have taken place in the same time period. Babies have been sent from Canada to fill adoption placement needs in the United States. Canadians have grown up thinking they were adopted, fully expecting to inherit the family farm or business, only to discover they had been casually accepted into the family and had no legal status.

This is a vast area of ignorance in a country that keeps exact count of the numbers of elk roaming the Northland.

Partly this lack of knowledge about the adopted population stems from the fact that the various provinces enacted legislation at different times and, therefore, began to keep ˇ statistics at different times. There are inconsistencies in the way provinces record statistics for the various kinds of adoptions: private adoptions, agency adoptions, and family adoptions (where the stepfather adopts children of his wife's earlier marriage, for example).

Another reason for the lack of knowledge is that, until recently, nobody asked. Agencies considered adoption over and done with on completion of the adoptive process (completion in the professional/legal view, that is). After that it was only the business of the adopting parents. Adoptees did not dare raise questioning heads. Professionals moved into research about adoption late in the game. Consequently, only now are annual adoption statistics being pulled out of musty departmental reports to be tallied.

b. SEALED RECORDS

Whatever the reason for your search, the custom of sealing original birth records will be your greatest obstacle to success. You cannot obtain, unless laws are changed, your original birth certificate with your biological identity, which was "sealed" and replaced with an amended version to suit your adopted status.

This means that unlike other citizens, an adopted adult is unable to obtain original birth records or adoption records. This is the obstacle you face in attempting to uncover your roots.

The "as if" concept, and the secrecy required to preserve this type of created relationship, are protected by this sealing of records.

For instance, the Child Welfare Act of Manitoba states:

> 92. All records and documents in the office of a child caring agency related to the granting of an order of

adoption shall be confidential and following the granting of the order shall be maintained in a separate file and secured in a locked fire-proof vault by the child caring agency.

93. A file maintained in accordance with section 92 shall not be opened for inspection except

(a) by the director of child welfare, or on his written order, or

(b) by the executive director of the agency wherein the file is secured; or

(c) on the order of a judge of the Court of Queen's Bench, a Surrogate Court, or a County Court.

94. All records and documents related to the granting of an order of adoption in a County Court shall be confidential, and no search of such records or making of any coies thereof or extracts therefrom shall be permitted except under an order made by a judge of the Court of Queen's Bench, Surrogate Court or County Court after reasonable notice for that purpose is given to the director.

Legislation in other provinces and in most states of the United States is similar, with courts guarding the original identity of adopted persons.

Most adoption statutes do provide for the opening up of sealed records by court order or on the written direction of the Director of Child Welfare. However, it is a provision rarely used, and it is not there to help you find your origins, but to cover such probabilities as marriage of blood relatives or questions concerning succession to property.

Sealing, or locking up, the original birth certificate is a custom that affects millions of people in North America: the adopted and their original and adoptive parents, and the numerous siblings, grandparents, and other relatives. In the United States there are estimated to be more than a million adult adopted people and several million adopted children.

"For decades our profession has insisted on the sealing of records relating to adoptions, without the benefit of any follow-up studies to support its policy," wrote Doris H. Bertocci, a social worker at Columbia University.

"It is now being forced to admit that the effects of sealing these records have been far more complicated than anyone ever would have imagined, for the administrators of agencies handling adoptions are presently caught in a cross-fire between angry adoptees on one hand and fearful workers and adoptive parents on the other."

Margaret E. Edgar, a Montreal social worker who founded the Open Door Society Inc., and who is an adoptive parent, explained the need for the facts of origins in this way:

> Should anyone, social worker, adopting parent, genetic or biological parent, or judge interpreting the law have the right to deny an individual knowledge about himself and his origins? Without diverging into a discussion on heredity versus environment in adoption, I am stating that heredity, the stock from which we come, does play a part in what we achieve even if the minimal contribution is our physique and physical appearance. It is part of our identity.

A growing number of adopted people, professionals in the field, and others in society, share this view and are striving to have sealed record legislation amended.

c. OPEN RECORDS
Some countries provide access to your original birth records, and the official information you can obtain helps in tracing your origins.

1. Scotland
The importance of biological identity was recognized in the Scottish Adoption Act of 1930. If you are over the age of 17 and were adopted in Scotland, you can write to:

Registrar General
New Register House
Edinburgh 2, Scotland

for a copy of your original birth certificate, which is obtainable by mail. Also ask the Registrar if there is any other information available, such as the name of the court or the agency (if any) that arranged the adoption.

Usually your original birth certificate includes the names of your parent(s), your original name, place and date of birth, the occupation of your natural parent(s), and their usual address at the time of your birth.

2. England and Wales

If you were born and adopted in England or Wales, the Children Act of 1975 gives you access to your original birth records and the linking information that will help you trace your origins. The law applies to adopted people over the age of 18. If you were adopted before November 12, 1975, an interview with a counsellor is required before any information can be supplied to you. This means that you would have to plan a trip overseas to appear in person for counselling if you are applying for information from North America. Counselling is optional for those adopted after November 12, 1975.

The purpose of counselling is to ensure that you have considered the possible effect of your enquiries, on yourself and others, and that the information is given to you in a helpful and appropriate manner. The counsellor does not have the right to withhold the basic information that will give you access to your birth records, even in the exceptional cases where the counsellor is worried about possible consequences.

The concluding paragraph of a publication entited *Access to birth records — Notes for counsellors* states that "Applicants are adult people with a right to make their own decisions about how much or how little information about their origins they want. It is also for them to decide how they use this information."

Applications for information are made to the Registrar-General; the address is in Appendix 3. The Children Act does not apply to Northern Ireland.

14

In some cases adopted adults who already had the names of their original parents have been able to obtain their original birth certificates by mail, without the required personal interview as stated above. When making an enquiry, be sure to give all the details in case an exception may be made in your case.

At present there are no arrangements for people to have their counselling interview outside Britain. The Association of British Adoption and Fostering Agencies, a charitable organization, reports that the Registrar General's office has been asked whether it would be legally and administratively possible to arrange such interviews overseas. Perhaps if all those who would like to obtain their original birth certificates write to the Registrar, the demand for overseas counselling service will bring about a change in policy.

"People whose adoption was arranged by an agency in Scotland, England or Wales should write to the agency direct if they wish to enquire whether there is background information on file," suggests Marilyn Ruber, assistant director, The Association of British Adoption and Fostering Agencies in London. "Our association can be of help in providing the current address of named agencies, but as each agency keeps its own files, and there is no central register, we are not able to tell people whether or not they were placed through an agency.

"However, if people whom the Registrar has been unable to help send us all the information or clues they have (*not* original documents, please) including places, names of court, religious persuasion, etc., we would do our best to suggest to them agencies which might have been involved, either in placing for adoption or making social reports to the court, etc., and then it would be up to the adopted people themselves to follow up any suggestions made."

When corresponding with the Association of British Adoption and Fostering Agencies, send an international reply coupon to cover the cost of reply postage. Enclose a coupon when writing to anyone outside of Canada with a request for information or assistance.

3. Finland

Adopted adults who were born in Finland also have access to their original birth records. Legislation in Finland does not recognize the principle of "adoptio incognito." The Population Act of January 1, 1971 gives every person born in Finland the right to obtain all information concerning origins from the official population records. From these records, according to Ritva HalmeKauranen, Legislative Counsellor, Ministry of Justice, an adopted person can, among other facts, learn the names of biological parents.

In theory, the relinquishing mother or the parents surrender the child directly to the adoptive parents. The name of the mother or the parents is given to the population register of the adoptive parents, and the biological parents' population register includes the name of adopting parents.

The child can inherit both from the adoptive parents and from the biological parents. The population register of the mother is asked to keep the name of the adopting family confidential, but if the mother insists, she can get it. Most mothers and most adopted people in Finland, however, do not seek the available information, according to Save the Children, the largest and only private adoption agency in Finland.

A biological mother wishing later to know about her child can get in touch with Save the Children, which is named in the court minutes, and make enquiries. The agency will try to obtain a picture of the child from the adoptive parents, if the mother wants one, as part of its ongoing casework with the mother, but it does not co-operate on a request for a personal contact before the adoptee is 20 years of age. At that time, if the adoptee refuses to have contact with the mother, the decision is respected.

Save the Children handles about 45% of the 550 or so adoptions in Finland each year, and receives requests for information about origins from about 50 to 70 adopted people annually.

"We see this aspect of our work as an essential part of our adoption service," said Dr. Elina Rautenan. "Our follow-up service, when needed, gives every kind of help and support the adoptee needs. We usually make the connection with the parents. It is part of our casework service."

"When birth parents are reluctant to have contact with grown children, some kind of compromise is usually made," she said. "Our agency was the first in the world to begin a follow-up service for adoptees, 25 years ago."

Finland's adoption legislation came into force in 1925 and the agency then began to systematically preserve as much information as possible in adoption files to be ready to answer questions in future.

Save the Children offers ongoing casework service to all parties in the adoption triad. Some adoptees go to the agency on their own for answers to puzzling questions, but sometimes they come with adoptive parents. The case-worker attempts to discover what the stress or special situation was that promoted the visit. The agency needs to see the situation as a whole in order to be of service, as Dr. Rautenan wrote:

> What do we tell the young people who come to us? I think they are entitled to know all about their background. The situation may be difficult for the social worker. Perhaps it is due to our training that we would want to protect our client from the knowledge of real rejection, abandonment, social squalor and disease, particularly mental disease. However, in this kind of work it is not possible, and we may not even be able to stop the client from coming into direct contact with such circumstances. Also, we have learned through experience that it is no use trying to make things 'nicer' for everyone. The only thing we can do is to try to

understand reality and to interpret this understanding to the client.

The adoptee's desire to know about origins may be threatening to the adoptive parents and the agency takes the time to serve them as well. The biological mother becomes part of the situation when an adoptee wishes to meet her. The agency has found that the mother's attitude and behavior to a great extent are influenced by her feelings and situation when she gave up her child. She requires help to live through the process of separation and to accept the guilt feelings which are an inevitable part of the separation where she has taken the initiative, for otherwise she will be badly prepared to meet her son or daughter in later years.

When work with the mother has been inadequate, or when she is unable to face the situation of giving up the child realistically, she may deny the existence of the child or tell people that she was persuaded to give up her baby. In most cases, both the biological mother and the adoptee are very much involved with their own problems when they meet and permanent ties are seldom established following reunion.

"We think that it would be best if all these meetings could be prepared by the social agency which took care of the placement," Dr. Rautenan wrote. "A social worker could then explain to both parties their feelings about each other and about themselves."

The agency has learned from experience that the adoptive placement is not an isolated event, but one phase in a dynamic process in the child's life. All participants have a continuous influence on the process, all of them develop and change, and the agency should be there to meet the critical situations which may arise, ready for those participants of the process who may ask for its help.

3

THE ADOPTED SPEAK UP

a. THE ADOPTEES' RIGHTS MOVEMENT

For most of the history of modern adoption practice in North America it was assumed by professionals and the public that a good adoptive home would dispel the adopted person's need for information about origins. If a "chosen" person went back to an agency with searching questions about biological identity — and until recently it took a great deal of courage to do so — the questions were considered a sign of emotional disturbance. Given that professional bias, adoptive parents tended to feel they had failed when the adopted child became seriously interested in origins.

In 1953, Jean M. Paton-Kittson, an adopted person and a professional social worker, interviewed adopted people for a study on their need for biological connections, and pioneered the movement for change.

She had a master's degree in economics and statistics from the University of Wisconsin, and a master's degree from the University of Pennsylvania School of Social Work, when she decided to discover whether adopted people had anything to say. Her work was reported in a book entitled *The Adopted Break Silence*. She continued her work with adopted people through Orphan Voyage, an organization she founded in Cedaridge, Colorado.

Jean Paton-Kittson searched for and found her mother when she was 47 and her natural mother was 69. She believes that "in the soul of every orphan is an eternal flame of hope for reunion and reconciliation with those he has lost through private or public disaster."

She writes that adoptees are always considered adopted children and never become true adults in the eyes of society. She has suggested the concept of a reunion registry in which information could be recorded on adopted persons and their natural parents, so that when the adoptee is an adult a reunion could be arranged if either party so desired and both sides were mutually agreeable.

Over the years since 1953, adoption began to come out of the closet for public discussion; other self-help groups were formed in a grass roots movement to change adoption legislation to assist adopted people in their search for origins.

b. GROUPS THAT WILL HELP YOU

1. Parent finders

Parent finders is a non-profit self-help movement that was founded by three adoptees in August, 1974. Joan Vanstone, Gary Cowley and Shannon Blomberg happened to be looking for their background stories at the same time and met after they had gone to the Children's Aid Society in Vancouver for information.

The late Honor Mowinckel, a social worker who was familiar with the pioneer work of Jean Paton-Kittson in the United States, invited them to an agency seminar on adoption. Afterward they were able to discuss their common frustration about the lack of helpful information available at the agency and, encouraged by Mowinckel, they organized a meeting for adoptees, and Parent Finders was born.

Since then the movement has spread from coast to coast, with groups in cities and towns, and a reunion registry for adopted adults and birth relatives has been established. Assistance and advice is provided, on request, to adopted people over the age of majority (usually 18 years old) in the province in which they reside, and an intermediary service is available for a reunion approach.

All assistance and support is given by volunteers who themselves have completed a search and are willing to help others in need. The group in British Columbia is further assisted by the professional experience of a social worker who acts as volunteer counsellor.

Fees are kept low and no one is refused help because of an inability to pay.

Shannon Blomberg's story, told on radio and in the newspapers, helped to bring Parent Finders to the attention of the public. She knew about her adoption from the age of four. She was raised in an affluent home, but her adoptive parents died when she was ten and she spent the next sixteen years searching for her natural family. She wrote pleading letters to child welfare officials, took jobs in special places such as hospitals, in the hope of finding her birth records, and at one point employed a detective agency. Shannon found her birth mother, despite the fact that her mother had changed her first name and had a new married surname.

"We both have problems," she told a reporter after the reunion. "She is suffering from guilt. I am suffering from rejection. But we both have a sense of humor. If we hadn't, it would be a heavy relationship."

She was accepted by her mother and by her mother's husband, who had not known about Shannon previously, but was not identified to friends. Feeling bound by a commitment made to her mother not to contact her natural father, Shannon has seen him frequently in the office building where she is employed, but has not approached him.

Gary Cowley, another founder of Parent Finders, is a businessman in the Lower Mainland of British Columbia, with a wife and family. His natural mother had died by the time he found her identity, but he found a half-brother with whom he has a friendly relationship.

"We all make excuses why we want to find these people," he said. "To me, it's because they are there."

2. Reunion Registry

The Reunion Registry maintained by Parent Finders is open to any adult adopted person, natural parent, or other birth relative, who wishes to be registered. A fee ($10 in 1978) is charged, and members also receive assistance with searching, group support and a newsletter. An intermediary service is available if desired.

If you were born in Canada but live elsewhere, or your child was born in Canada and you live elsewhere, you may be listed in the registry. Anyone wishing to be listed should write or call one of the Parent Finders groups, or contact the national office in Vancouver (addresses are listed in Appendix 2) for an application form. The form has spaces for the particulars that will be entered in the registry, such as your name, place and date of birth, and where you can be contacted.

Not everyone who asks to be entered in the Reunion Registry is conducting a search. Some people wish to be listed to signify their willingness to be found and contacted should the other party undertake a search. All information is considered confidential. Parent Finders looks forward to the day when this register can be handled by government ministries as part of provincial adoption services.

3. Reunion File

Orphan Voyage in the United States maintains a registry called Reunion File, which allows for matching up of information supplied by both parties seeking a reunion.

Active membership in Orphan Voyage is open to all adult members of the adoption population and to others affected by sealed records. The fee for the first year is $20, and this covers inclusion in the Reunion File, if desired; use of intermediary services; referral to individuals and groups, correspondence during search; and the newsletter, LOG. (LOG by itself is available for $5 on a one-year trial basis.)

Members of groups affiliated with Orphan Voyage pay a $10 membership fee for the same full services, and renewals are $10 a year. Agencies and professionals pay $10 a year.

Birth parents and adoptive parents of adoptees under the age of 18 are eligible for membership and may use the Reunion File. When birth and adoptive parents of an adoptee are matched through the file, it is assumed they are prepared for communication in the interest of the adoptee. Adoptees under the age of 18 may use the registry with the encouragement of their adoptive parents. They pay no fee, but the LOG is sent to the adoptive parents who are expected to become members.

4. Yesterday's Children

Yesterday's Children is a non-profit organization in the United States dedicated to the proposition that all adults have a right to knowledge of their own historical past. Most members have been separated from biological families through foster care or adoption, divorce, or the death of parents, and knowledge of origins has been lost to them. The group is actively working to amend state laws on record disclosure.

"It is not the conviction of the membership of Yesterday's Children that adoption and foster care are, of themselves, wrong," said Donna Cullom, president. "But it is our belief that these relationships have been gravely damaged and unhappily burdened by the attempt to destroy the evidence of the child having any existence before his separation and relocation. We believe that the success and mutual satisfaction in any relationship depends upon honesty, openness and trust. While it may meet adult needs to structure foster and adoptive family relationships to exclude other parents and a different biological heritage, it does not meet the needs of the people to whom it is done."

Adopted adult members receive the assistance of a personal search assistant during search, who only guides and assists, and a newsletter. The membership fee is $25 per year.

Members are automatically listed in the group's National Adoption Registry of birth parents and adoptees. People who do not wish to join Yesterday's Children but would like to be entered in the registry may do so for a one-time fee of $5.

5. Alma

"Alma," a name derived from the Spanish word "alma" which means "soul," is the Adoptees' Liberty Movement Association, with headquarters in New York, New York, and affiliated groups in many states. Alma offers a reunion registry, mutual assistance in search, and search workshops, and it is striving to have legislation changed.

On May 23, 1977, Alma filed a class action suit in Federal District Court, Manhattan, challenging as unconstitutional New York's sealed records laws in regard to adult adoptees.

"When Alma's suit reaches the United States Supreme Court, and, we are fully prepared to take it there, a decision, though technically limited to declaring unconstitutional only the New York law, will have the effect, as a precedent, of invalidating similar laws in *all* other States. The decision will affect adoptees' rights everywhere," Alma president Florence Fisher said.

Alma's international reunion registry, soon to be computerized, is maintained at Alma headquarters in New York. Membership dues are $25 annually and include entry in the registry.

6. Jigsaw International

Jigsaw International is a non-profit self-help organization affiliated with Parent Finders Canada and 27 similar organizations in the United States. Adoptees, natural parents and adoptive parents may join for an initial fee of $15 and an annual fee of $15 a year. The head office is in Sydney, Australia, and there are five branches in Australia and another in New Zealand.

"Our usual method of operation is to assist the members as much as possible in their search and when the natural parent has been found the matter is put into the hands of the executive, who make the initial contact," explained Joanne Hile, president. "We have had over one hundred reunions in the two years we have been in operation. We are in the process of compiling a list to help members do their own searching."

Jigsaw International has a contact register to assist in matching up adoptees and natural mothers. The organization is lobbying the federal and state governments to change adoption laws to allow for access to birth certificates and social welfare files.

7. Assistance in the United Kingdom

If you are having a difficult time searching for roots in the United Kingdom, CONTACT may be able to help you. CONTACT is an organization designed to put people in touch with each other, providing both parties are over the age of 18 years.

There is a fee of three pounds if you merely wish to add your name to the reunion register. The fee is payable per year, and if the relative you seek is also registered, CONTACT will act as a third party to effect a meeting, but addresses of both parties remain anonymous unless they themselves wish to exchange them at reunion. Along with registration you will receive an advice sheet with some points to think over before embarking on your search.

CONTACT also has independent researchers who will assist you with searching records for a fee, which can be as little as 30 pounds plus the cost of a document for each entry found.

4

WHAT YOU SHOULD KNOW BEFORE YOU BEGIN SEARCHING

a. THE CHANCES FOR SUCCESS

As an adopted adult, you will begin your search for roots with a fairly cold trail, and the time required to warm it up depends on the amount of information with which you start out. You already know that some unfortunate circumstance is connected with your birth.

The circumstances vary and are such as might be found in human family research undertaken by anyone, so it is wise not to jump to conclusions. After wondering for years why you were given up for adoption you may find in tracing your roots that there is a logical explanation for this action. Once you know, it is easier to accept.

But how do you unravel the mystery and find your roots? Resourceful people, who have a deep need to know their origins and who are prepared to dig patiently for the facts, manage to overcome mighty obstacles.

It is not always possible to successfully trace your roots, but usually it is possible to know a little more than you did in the beginning, and that is a comfort. You may discover that your natural parents have died, but at least you know something about them.

You may find them alive and ready to share family history with you, as has been the experience of many searchers, or you could face unwelcome rejection. When this occurs you must accept it, however difficult, remembering that people are not computers that can be tapped automatically for a print-out of information. Sometimes they need time before feeling ready to co-operate. Patience, as Franz Kafka once said, is the master key to every situation.

"A fundamental defect in the law as it relates to children," J. Victor Belknap, British Columbia's Superintendent of Child Welfare, said recently, "is that children have no standing in the law. Right now if anything, children are objects rather than persons. In the adoption process a legal contract takes place between some parties, the relinquishing and adopting parents. The child is not seen to be a party to that."

But even though you were not party to the contract or information and your records are sealed and unavailable, you may have some snippets of knowledge that eventually will help you find your roots. Your adoptive parents may have some facts which they may be willing to give you. Indeed, some adoptive parents become so interested they share in the search.

Unfortunately, others, preoccupied with the concept of possession or fearful of losing love, either refuse to help or can't even be approached. You will know instinctively the situation in your case.

The support and assistance of a self-help group, like Parent Finders, can make your task easier.

While such groups can be helpful, you as an adoptee who has given this some careful thought, must decide for yourself whether to trace your roots. Not all adoptees wish to search. If you would like to meet natural relatives, a mutual decision involving the other party or parties will be required.

b. THE FOUR STAGES OF SEARCH

By the time you are ready to begin searching you have given the matter much thought, for a search develops in four stages.

The first stage is an internal process that can begin in late childhood or the early teen years, except for those who do not learn of their status until much later. All teenagers go through the turmoil of inner questioning and re-evaluation of the people close to them, as they pinch and prod and plump their self-image like sculptors at work with clay.

The adopted teenager has the added problem of knowing that another set of parents exists out there, somewhere.

Faceless people on an unmapped landscape. The mystery swirls about at the edges or centre of emotions already taxed to cope with body and attitude changes that can be confusing enough in themselves.

The second stage is a paper search, carried out with much excitement and creativity and characterized by some depression during blocks in progress and periods of inactivity or indecision.

Contact with original parents, siblings or others is made in the third stage. It is never easy to make this contact. Most searchers agonize over this step for varying lengths of time until the moment comes when they are ready. It is something like leaping off a cliff, because you don't know how you will be received and you want to be psychologically ready for rejection or acceptance. Putting it off resolves nothing, so finally the contact is made, either personally or through an intermediary.

This step may be followed by a reunion visit at a mutually arranged time. The third stage involves much thought and worry, followed by much activity in the contact and reunion phase.

This is the high point of the search, the climax to perhaps months and years of hard work, and surprisingly, very often the people contacted seem to have been expecting such a call at some time. "I was thinking about you a lot lately," some original parents say. Or, "I knew you'd call some day." Others confirm facts but need time to work out their concerns about the reactions of immediate family members or decide whether to tell them at all. A minority want no contact.

The first telephone contact between a searcher and found relative can go on for more than an hour, even at long distance rates, and afterward the adopted adult is keyed up and needs to tell someone else about it. This is when it helps to have an understanding volunteer to call, someone who will listen and listen for as long as it takes to "talk down," unwind and relax.

You can't believe that you actually talked with a relative, a parent or whoever, and you have to keep going over what was said and how it felt, absorbing the reality of this unique experience. Searchers who report on a contact call at a self-help group meeting often go into every detail at length. "I checked the number, I dialed, and I heard the ring, wondering if anyone would answer," they say. Every second of the experience is remembered as being important.

Then there are all the arrangements to make for the reunion itself, finding a time and a place which suits everyone. This can be the same day, several weeks later or months later, depending on the circumstances and the people.

The fourth stage of search begins after the reunion when the excitement wears off and you start trying to assimilate your identity as an adopted person and your emerging identity so that you come out as one complete person. We all play different roles at work, at home, and so on, and now in addition to your role with your adoptive parents you have to develop a role with natural parents. Even if you don't see the latter often, or hardly ever, you still must work this out in your own mind until everything fits comfortably. There is some exhaustion and disappointment in this stage during the effort to establish new relationships and the merging of adoptive and biological identities. This stage is made even more difficult when a spouse or others in the immediate family display their feelings of desertion, brought on by the searcher's concentration on the search and follow-up details.

c. YOUR REACTIONS TO THE SEARCH

The post-reunion period is a stage of adjustment, of slowly allowing new facts of origins to sift into your being, and to connect everything with the rest of your life. As for a light cake, fold ingredients in gently. Take your time. It may be that during this time you will have to come to terms with any disappointment that may follow reunion, especially if unrealistic expectations have been treasured for many years.

You may wonder whether to try to bring your adoptive and original parents together, or what to call various people. Generally, the adoptive mother continues to be called "Mom" or "Mother" and the natural mother is addressed by her first name. It does not seem to be a problem. Adopted people tend to speak of their first parents and their second parents, and seem more content having two kinds of parents whom they know about than in having to wonder about an unknown set of mystery parents.

Aside from the sharing of experiences offered in adoptee activist groups, there is not much help available elsewhere for searchers in coping with these stages.

"Social workers have not been trained to understand this process," Ben Eide said. "It is something no professional education school I know of has ever attempted to deal with. Professional education in adoption and child welfare are absolutely nil."

For some people these four stages are spread out over a long period of their life, while for others it is a process compressed into a short time. Sometimes the first and second stages almost blend together. Sandra, an only adopted child, knew there was something to be known other than the fact that she was adopted, and at age 12, while her parents were away, she found her adoption order and calmly copied every word on a sheet of paper that she preserved carefully for many years.

She did not reactivate stage two of her search until she was an adult, finding her natural father within eight months. "Hi, sweetheart," he responded when she called him by telephone at his office in another city. Although he preferred to withhold the news from his wife and children for the time being, he quickly flew to Sandra's city for a reunion visit and answered his daughter's many questions.

Her mother, who had married twice, was harder to find, but in time Sandra completed her search and felt satisfied. For some people stage two is picked up, dropped, and picked up again many times, a few more clues being added each time, before it is finally resolved.

The post-reunion fourth stage can go on for a year or two, one step at a time. Gradually life returns to a normal level, except that it has been expanded and now it seems perfectly natural to have in your life new friendships with original relatives as well as an adoptive family, and an ancestral history that has been woven into your life tapestry.

d. YOUR FAMILY'S REACTION TO THE SEARCH

Human relationships are fragile and must be tended with care, never more so it seems than when you are filled with the joy of having found people connected with your origins. Suddenly you may sense, if not outright disinterest, some sign of unhappiness in those closest to you. You who are so happy expect your loved ones to share in this hard-earned pleasure.

It may be beyond them. You may feel as if you are walking on eggs in your attempt not to ruffle anyone's feelings. Not only do you have the work of learning to know the people you have found (if you have proceeded to that stage), and their likes and dislikes, but you may have to cope with adoptive parents who are on edge or children who simply don't care, or spouses who feel they have lost your total interest. Never mind that you have had to share them with *their* relatives for years.

You will have to give everyone time to adjust to the new realities. One couple without children or relations actually separated temporarily when one spouse searched for and found original relatives. Previously, husband and wife had been totally dependent upon each other. There was no one else in their lives. This narrow existence obviously was not enough for the one who found a family. Fortunately the one who felt rejected was able to accept the situation eventually and the marriage survived on a new basis.

Even several years of correspondence with relatives may not be long enough for a spouse to remember who is who. There is a loud message in a casual "Who's that?" response to a letter from a relative whose name has been mentioned many times. This does not always happen, but it does happen.

Some families start out being indifferent to a search but warm up to it during the process when they see what it means to you. With some people you wonder if they will ever understand.

5
HOW TO SEARCH FOR YOUR ROOTS

a. IT'S UP TO YOU

"Please tell my daughter her baby picture is still on my dresser where it's been for 24 years" — birth mother to an intermediary making initial contact for an adoptee.

Now that you know something about adoption, the adoptees' rights movement, the stages of search and reunion, you want to get on with the central topic, which is finding your own lost roots. But knowing what you are dealing with is helpful, especially if your search is one of those that takes a long time. It could be over in a few days, if you are lucky, or could take months or even years. Successful searchers are patient and persistent.

Only you know on which day you will begin an active search. Once you have reached the stage of active search, success depends on the kind of facts with which you begin, for without some hard data a search is somewhat like trying to sail to a destination in a strange sea without a compass. It may be possible, but it is more difficult and requires more work and time.

b. WHERE TO BEGIN

Take stock of what you know to start with, writing down all the facts you have about yourself and your original parents. If you know your birth name, your parents' names, where you were born and where you were adopted, you have much more information than many searchers have initially. If you do not have any of this information, or only part of it, obtaining these facts will be your first task.

1. Talk to your adoptive parents

Your adoptive parents may be your first and best source of information and support. Many adoptive parents do not know the names of your original parents any more than you do and can't help with this information even if they would like to do so.

Some do have vital facts but can't be approached or, if approached, do not wish to discuss the matter. Some have dismissed the facts from mind, or say that both birth parents died. The story of birth parents who were both killed in an accident soon after their child was born is commonly heard.

If you do have problems discussing your need to know with adoptive parents, try to maintain a perspective, realizing that for some adoptive parents, who want to think of you as their own birth child (now grown) and to deny the very existence of original parents, answering your questions can be difficult.

But, if it is at all possible (and you will know this instinctively), discuss your need for knowledge about origins with your adoptive parents and try to enlist their support in your quest. A mutually shared search actually strengthens the bond of an adoptive relationship, and when this happens, as it does, it is a joy to behold. In some cases only one adoptive parent is approachable and shares in the search.

Adopted adults who fear or know that their adoptive parents would be hurt or alarmed by questions about their origins often decide either to search quietly on their own, or postpone active search until they feel free to do so. This may not be until they are in their thirties or forties.

If your adoptive parents are reluctant to impart information or are deceased, other members of your adoptive family may be willing and able to assist you. You will know what is possible, but don't assume too quickly that no one will want to discuss the matter.

There may be useful information stored in your memory, which you have not consciously thought about for years. Sit down and think back as far as you can. Old

34

memories may not come at once, but suddenly you will remember something, if only vaguely, that may be of importance.

2. Get background information

In most Canadian provinces the provincial adoption office will provide, on written request, all the non-identifying background information that is available for you. (See Appendix 1 for details.) In Ontario this information should be requested from the Children's Aid Society that arranged your adoption.

Usually this non-identifying information is typed up and described as a background sheet; it may provide some general information about your first parents and grandparents, such as the type of work they did, whether they lived in a city, town or rural area, ethnic origin, and so on. It can take from several weeks to more than a month to obtain a background sheet, as someone on the staff must cull the information from your file and put it all together and have it typed. Unless this is considered high priority work, it will take a back seat to more urgent business or routines.

If you receive scanty information it may be that your file is pretty bare, the person assembling the information may not be sympathetic to your quest or may be overworked, or the office does not wish to encourage queries such as yours.

Make another request, pressing for more information, and if necessary ask again, and again. People have found that each time they asked they received a bit more information, proving that it was not all given to them the first time. You need not feel that you are putting anyone out. These offices operate on public funds, and you, a taxpayer as well as a client, are entitled to service as much as the other parties in adoption.

If the information you receive is vague, ask specific questions about medical history, ethnic origin, and so on.

If you end up feeling that you have not been served, or that the staff gave you the impression you had no business to ask, do not waste energy becoming upset with an individual. Direct reasonable protests to the head of your provincial welfare office, the local member of your legislature, the cabinet minister responsible for adoption, the attorney general, the premier and the provincial or state human rights organization, and all equivalent U.S. people.

The quality of your background sheet will depend, in part, on how much information was obtained and recorded in the beginning. Try to picture what was happening to your original parents at the time. Relinquishment of a child for adoption is a traumatic situation, a time when the person is caught up in a torrent of emotions as attempts are made to deal with a serious life problem in a way that ensures survival.

Your birth mother likely was going through heavy pressure and shame, having to think about plans for you and also her future. Birth mothers have recalled at public meetings in recent years how they were pressured constantly by social workers or their own mothers to sign consent for adoption to the point where they felt totally confused. They were told how much more others could do for their babies and that if they really loved them they would sign. SIGN.

Only later did they realize how very final the step was and how fully they were cut out of their child's life, and it is this part, the total severance, that bothered them over the years. They say they did want to assure the child would have a good and stable life with loving adoptive parents, but they wanted to know later if that was the outcome, if their child was doing well or even alive. Many went back to agencies tormented by the questions, and learned nothing.

Others tried to put it all out of their minds, successfully severing the ties.

Relinquishing mothers have been known, under stress, to use fictitious names — and if they didn't think of it, often someone else did — in an effort to expunge the truth. In some provinces babies of unwed mothers were routinely baptized, for a time, with false names used for that purpose; one name for boys, another for girls, as, for example, Joseph Du Bois and Marie Du Bois.

Use of numbers on all but the sealed documents, which contain your real name, is another practice that may complicate your search. Often the birth father (called the putative father by social agencies) was listed as unknown. This is how your best interests have been handled.

Fortunately, Catholic mothers have tended to insist on baptism prior to relinquishment and usually a priest from a nearby church is available for baptism. Locate the church nearest the place of your birth and write to the priest with a request for a copy of your baptismal records. Should he be the wrong parish priest, try the next nearest church. Protestant churches usually also are co-operative in providing copies of baptismal records that are requested for use in family scrapbooks or family histories. Elaborating further on your reasons for requesting the information may not be to your advantage.

Should false names complicate your search you would need some other facts to go on, unless someone in your original family has registered in a reunion registry in which you are registered. Not only would you then know that person wants to be found, but you might find each other through the matching of facts. For example, if a mother who gave up a daughter born March 10, 1932 at Ottawa General Hospital and a woman with similar information turns up in a register, chances are good that they are mother and daughter. It then becomes a matter of ascertaining identities for a fact.

Today, illegitimate birth is not quite the horror it once was and the need for elaborate cover-up is not as strong. At one time the unwed mother risked being ostracized by family and community, taking the brunt of responsibility for an act that required two people, and, consequently, a web of secrecy was devised to protect her and her child from shame.

If you find that false names were used in your case, it's wise to remember the times and atmosphere. But even if you do not wish to have the protection that stems from the system, you still have to work your way through the web to get at the facts.

Now that social workers and agencies are aware of the possibility that information will be sought in future by grown adopted people, a greater attempt is being made to secure accurate background information. Some social workers say that they try to interview the birth mother's mother for as much information as can be obtained about family history.

Earlier, information was recorded not for the purpose of giving it to you, the adult adopted person, but for the purpose of matching adoptable children with adopting parents of similar appearance and other likeness. Nobody expected you to come asking for this information.

3. Read your background information

Read any background information you obtain carefully. It may tell you, for example, that your grandfather was a grocer in a small town and your birth mother was an only child who worked in the store on Saturdays until she completed school or dropped out of high school. Grandmother had arthritis and an aunt lived with the family, helping with the work.

Already some pieces of your incomplete jigsaw puzzle are falling into place, and questions are being answered. You may not care for the answers. Take time to mull over the information and try to assimilate it.

Illegitimacy is not worn comfortably at first and if you find this is part of your history and had not suspected it, remember that this is only another way of coming into the world and has been happening since time immemorial. Kings have been born in the same circumstances. You may notice some interesting reference in your background information about hair and eye coloring, height, or other facts that help to bring those first parents to life for you.

This may be enough, but if you decide you need to know more, look for the route in your background sheet. The small town grocery store operated by your grandfather, in this example, may be traceable if you can zero in on the right town in the right province or state. It won't be easy, but it could lead you to more definite information about the key people you wish to contact.

Search, as you can see, often is travel on a dark, uncharted continent and requires courage and infinite patience.

4. Find out who, where and when
During your search, always try to obtain full given names in order to positively identify people. Don't assume anything. After spending months tracing an individual from his prairie birthplace to his grave on the West Coast, I discovered he was the wrong person, although related. I should have been tracing a person whose name was similar except for a middle name. Time wasted, money wasted, all because I ignored a warning signal in that middle name.

Dates and places are important to your genealogical search. If you learn that a person you are tracing died "about 15 years ago," try to pinpoint the date exactly by applying for a certificate of death from the appropriate office of vital statistics. You can pay an additional fee for a search of a group of years, when you do not have the exact year. Establishing identification is much easier, besides being more accurate, if you have exact birth, marriage and death dates. Other important dates could be those applying to immigration, military service, divorce, or baptism.

Set up a file for these documents. In fact, keep all data obtained in file folders, in an orderly fashion, so that you can find anything you need when you need it.

When applying for public documents, simply request them as anyone else would, and enclose the required fee. It is not necessary to go into a long explanation about your adoption, etcetera.

Once you have a positive date of death of one of your ancestors, you can go to microfilm in a public library and look for a newspaper obituary notice, which will give you additional information.

c. DOING LIBRARY RESEARCH
1. Public libraries

Libraries are an invaluable source of assistance in any genealogical research. If you live near a good, metropolitan library so much the better. But even when you must rely on research by mail or require information from a library in a small community, you are more than likely to receive courteous, helpful response — especially if you are courteous enough to include a cheque to cover the cost of any photocopying required and a self-addressed, stamped return envelope.

City directories dating back many years, telephone directories for a whole region, for other cities and often other countries are housed in libraries. There are also business and professional directories and newspaper clipping files that often can be useful.

Librarians, by and large, are happy to assist, especially in small town libraries where they not only have the library resources but also often know about community oldtimers and perhaps even their living descendants. There ought to be a national "take your librarian to lunch week," for without librarians all genealogical work and many other pursuits would be in jeopardy.

Before going off to a library to do research, make notes of the information to be checked out and take along a notebook in which to record your findings. When you arrive, if it is your first visit, take time to familiarize yourself with where things are kept. The librarian will be happy to help you in this. Discovering from the start where indexes relating to genealogy are filed could save many wasted hours. There is always a chance you might find an ancestor written up in one of the published genealogies at the library.

The Library of Congress in Washington, D.C., has copies of thousands of American and foreign genealogies. Ask for free leaflets describing these by writing to:

General Reference and Bibliography Division
Library of Congress
Washington, D.C. 20540

Ask whether your library has collections of old newspapers, either bound or on microfilm. By looking up an ancestor's obituary, you will pick up the names of other relatives. You may be looking for a sister who has married and seems impossible to trace because you don't know her married surname. It may be waiting for you in a relative's obituary.

2. Church libraries

One of the best library resources in North America is the Genealogical Library of the Church of Jesus Christ of the Latter-Day Saints, with headquarters in Salt Lake City, Utah. The Canadian branches of this library are listed here:

Alberta
    2021 — 17th Avenue, S.W.
    Calgary, Alberta

    348 Third Street
    Cardston, Alberta

    9010 - 85th Street
    Edmonton, Alberta

    2410 — 28th Street, South
    Lethbridge, Alberta

British Columbia
    5280 Kincaid Street
    Burnaby, British Columbia

    Glenmore & Ivans Street
    Kelowna, British Columbia

Ontario
    95 Melbert Street
    Etobicoke, Ontario

Each branch has equipment for reading the microfilm records, and through it you have access to the main library in Salt Lake City, which houses the greatest genealogical collection in the world.

This equipment can be ordered on loan at a reasonable price from the main library. Microfilm records are available from many countries, on a variety of subjects. There are records on birth, marriage and death registrations, census records, land registrations, town descriptions, and so on, up to certain points in time.

The best way to use the church library is to make a visit for the purpose of acquainting yourself with the type of information that is available. These libraries are staffed by dedicated volunteers who, like their church, take genealogy seriously and are most helpful. They believe that the church's "sealing ordinance," which is concerned with the obligation to be sealed to one's dead relatives as well as to the living, is the capstone of all ordinances of the church. Their book, *Genealogy of the Dark Continent*, explains the responsibility of "sealing" and the importance of being certain that one is sealed to the proper people, who are identified through systematic research.

If you have an idea that an ancestor was born in England, for example, around a certain time, you could order a microfilm of the birth, death and marriage register for that year, or a number of years, on the chance of picking up the name you have. Beside the name will be the volume number and page number of the register in which the birth, marriage or death was recorded. Armed with that data, you can then write to the registry office in London for a copy of the certificate required.

It was while studying microfilm one day in the hope of finding an ancestor born in the 1800's, that I came across another person of the same family name and area in the marriage register. Naturally, I made note of the volume and page numbers, which was a good thing, because he turned out to be my natural grandfather. I had not found the birth listing that was the reason for my visit to the library, but my grandfather's history materialized! In due course I knew also about his wife, my grandmother, and since have acquired an old photograph of that sturdy matriarch, who mothered a large family and worked hard to the end of her life, dying in her late eighties.

Microfilm from the Canadian Archives also is available at the Genealogical Library.

3. Foreign libraries

Libraries in other countries sometimes will assist you with research. The National Library of Ireland, for a fee, will help you trace ancestors. Other national libraries and genealogy societies are helpful and some are listed in Appendix 3.

District record offices are the best source, often, but require a personal visit for checking of old files as staff do not have the time to do your research for you.

4. Public Archives of Canada

The Public Archives of Canada were founded in 1872 and certain collections are available to genealogical researchers. A booklet on *Tracing Your Ancestors in Canada*, published by the Archives in 1972, warns that efforts to trace ancestors generally will not meet with success unless you can supply some details that narrow the search, such as the approximate birth and death dates, or place of residence. The Archives can make no effort to establish family relationships not clearly stated in the documents in their custody.

Sources for genealogical research in Canada include:

(a) Census records to 1871
(b) Vital statistics (provincial records of births, marriage and deaths)
(c) Land records
(d) Wills
(e) Notarial records
(f) Military records
(g) Immigration records

A checklist of parish registers available on microfilm also may be obtained from the Public Archives in Ottawa.

d. CHECKING DIRECTORIES

City directories can be immensely useful in tracing roots. If you were born in Toronto in 1940, for example, and you know your birth mother's name (or birth father's name), you could look in the city directory to see whether either was listed there that year or a few years before then. Whenever possible start checking directory listings five years prior to your birth. They might not have lived in Toronto at all. Try a directory for a community nearby.

If you do find a listing for your year of birth, check the directories of succeeding years until the listing for that name ends. You then have the last known address for that area, and you may find a neighbor who remembers the person and knows a more recent address.

Directories often list a place of employment or occupation, providing more clues to help you build a realistic picture of the person for whom you are searching. If you always dreamed of your birth mother as being beautiful and rich and you find her listed in a directory employed as a seamstress in a garment factory, you will have to revise your expectations rapidly. With two feet on the ground and a clear head you likely will decide that a living seamstress is far better than an impossible dream.

Life stories are spun out in directory listings when they are compiled over a period of years. Extract the name you are tracing from the directory pages, making up your own listing for that person, year by year until line by line the profile emerges. John Doe may first appear in the directory as a student living at home (jot down the parents' names as well), but a few years later is listed at another address with a wife who continues to be listed for five years before she disappears from the listing. What happened? Did she die? Were they separated? If the wife is the person you are looking for you would try to obtain the answers to those questions through further research (such as checking obituaries and divorce records of that time), but if you are mainly interested in John Doe you would not take the time and trouble for that. Doe may remarry or disappear from the directory pages as well, and your problem would be to discover what happened to him, using the last known occupation and address as your working clues.

Photocopy directory pages in your own library or request copies by mail, sending money to cover the copying cost and a stamped, self-addressed return envelope. Most libraries will copy three years of listings for a name at one time.

e. WRITING LETTERS

Every time you obtain a new fact it will lead you to search for more facts as your search progresses. Soon you will be writing letters of enquiry to *anyone* who seems likely to have some information, no matter how slight.

Purchase a supply of stamps and envelopes, because every letter of enquiry should go out with a stamped, self-addressed envelope for reply. If you are writing to someone out of the country, enclose an international postal coupon for reply. This is courteous and will encourage a reply.

Staple reply letters to your enquiry letters and keep them in file folders to avoid loss and confusion. You are conducting vital personal business, and going about it in a businesslike manner will protect you from feeling you are getting nowhere. One day you might feel that way, but a quick check through your files will prove that actually much more progress has been made.

Some of the replies you receive from strangers will warm your heart and give you courage. Most of my enquiry letters asked for information for a family history that I was preparing, and even when people could not supply answers they would add a note to wish me luck. One elderly gentleman advised me to start at the beginning and thoughtfully pointed out the great movement of people into and across Canada at the time about which I had enquired. This set me off on a whole new train of thought and helped me, in the end, discover that my parents had not only come to Canada but had left it.

The reason I wrote enquiry letters saying I was writing a family history project was that, in fact, I did plan to write my family history. But also I did not wish to describe these relationships to everyone. If you write to someone who did indeed know your birth parents, or one of them, but did not know that you were born and relinquished, you don't have to be the one who discloses this fact. Enquire discreetly.

Keep copies of the letters you mail out, so that if there is further correspondence you will know what was stated in your first letter.

f. FOLLOWING CLUES

Every little clue, no matter how insignificant it may seem, is worth follow-up. Ask a lot of questions, for you never know when a question will provide another clue. For example, you may find in checking old directories for a name you have that while *it* never appears, another name, similar in sound, does keep turning up. Perhaps only the first letter is different in the two names, so that instead of Karson, the name you were looking for, you keep finding Larson at the right time in the right place. This would be worth following up, just in case a change of name is complicating your search.

A clue to occupation is helpful and can be followed up by writing to the appropriate source of information. If you find a relative who is dead, the trail may not be as cold as you think. You can apply for a certificate of death to establish the date and place of death, then make enquiries locally regarding next of kin. Funeral notices or funeral homes can be helpful with this step. Voters lists also are useful in searching.

A small library may not have directories for the period of time you are interested in, but the librarian may tell you the name of an oldtimer in the area who might be able to assist you with the information you seek. Here is a lead that may provide a clue or two, for oldtimers enjoy recalling past years and would appreciate your interest.

Some clues undoubtedly will take you on side trips along dead-end roads. There is that risk of wasted time, but on the other hand, you might run into some interesting people.

g. NEWSPAPER ADVERTISEMENTS

When all else fails, you can place a newspaper advertisement in the area of search asking for information about the person you seek. You can insert your telephone number for collect calls, or use a box number. There is some nuisance risk in using your telephone number, as I discovered during my search when I received an early morning call from someone who claimed to know that the person I sought had died. Actually, the caller knew nothing about the person.

Perhaps that was unusual, for others have had better luck with advertisements. Gary Cowley, a founder of Parent Finders, for example, advertised during his search for his mother and received a call the next day from an aunt who told him his mother was dead but that he had two half-brothers on his mother's side. Next day he was having tea with his newly found aunt, seeing a blood relative for the first time in his life.

"I remember thinking that I'd finally found someone with the same big eyebrows and round face," he said. His aunt gave him a ring that had been his mother's and a picture of her.

If you advertise you ought to decide in advance what to say if someone calls, or writes to the box number, and asks why you want the information before giving you any. You have to play it by ear to a certain extent, for it may depend on who has the information. But generally speaking, a simple statement that you need the information in connection with a family matter is quite true and will suffice.

You can word advertisements in a variety of ways. One example is:

> Sam Seaker, last known residing in Wawanono in 1934 or anyone having knowledge of this person or present whereabouts, please call collect to (614) 222-1111.

A successful reunion followed publication of an advertisement like this in a Toronto newspaper:

> Laura Lost would like to hear from relatives. Box 999.

The woman who placed the advertisement used her birth name in the hope that her first mother would see it, which is exactly what happened. Her mother, who had never married and had no other children, was ecstatic and sent a reply to the box number at once.

h. ANCIENT HISTORY

Often old facts are easier to unearth than the more recent ones that you are most intent on finding, which is why you may end up visiting cemeteries to check out dates and names on old grave stones. If the cemetery is near enough to where you live, you can do this yourself; if not you may have to ask someone else to do it for you. Take along some talc to rub into very old inscriptions to make the lettering easier to read.

If your roots are deep in a country overseas, you can do research during a trip if that is possible, or contact the country's embassy in North America for the addresses of offices which can provide information.

In England, for example, the Public Record Office has a variety of records that can be helpful. There are many documents containing references to individuals and families emigrating to various colonies and places in different parts of the world, but there is no single index to the names of such persons. The Colonial Office and the Home Office have valuable papers, and there are many other sources of information, gems such as plantation records of the colonies and passenger lists from 1890.

In some cases a record agent may be engaged to search old records for you. Two such agents in England are:

Mr. P. N. Thompson
Ferndale Cottage
Christchurch
Coleford, Gloucester

Mr. K. Myers
4 Ravensbourne Close
Shoreham-by-Sea, Sussex

They charge a fee and you make your own arrangements with them.

6

HOW LONG WILL IT TAKE?

There is no way of knowing in advance how long a search will take. Some are wound up in a few days while others, like my own, drag on for years and are difficult to conclude.

Not long ago, a young man in British Columbia made up his mind to locate his birth mother before his scheduled flight to a university in eastern Canada. He arrived in Vancouver, accompanied by his adoptive mother, with only a few days to spare for his search. He had a strong feeling that he must find her before he left.

Fortunately for him, he had his birth mother's name and had an approximate idea of her age. As it turned out, she was located within a few days. She was living in a local nursing home. The young man, whom we'll call Ted, went to the home in the company of a volunteer helper from Parent Finders, where they spoke to the matron explaining Ted's quest. All information checked out and the matron was delighted. Ted's aging mother, chronically ill, was confined to a wheelchair and had long been depressed. Observing her, Ted was not at all sure he should speak to her. He was afraid it might upset her. Encouraged by the matron, he had a talk with his birth mother, who confirmed his facts but said little else. The son went away saddened.

Later in the day, Ted and his adoptive mother sent flowers to the home for his birth mother, and soon afterward the matron was in touch with him to ask whether he could return for another visit. His birth mother was anxious to see him. This time the blank expression was gone and the two enjoyed a genuine conversation. Ted was able to leave for his studies, feeling that he had brightened his birth mother's life.

That was a quick and happy search and reunion. Usually it takes longer. It can be because of the difficulty in obtaining information or because the adopted person, as frequently happens, picks up the search, adds a few stitches, and lays it down for a while. But it remains unfinished business and is not forgotten.

In my own case I did not know definitely of my adopted status until my late teen years, although by then I had long felt from the way things were at home and what was said that I somehow did not fit, that perhaps something was wrong with me.

My foster mother died when I was young and my father remarried. One day his wife screamed at me: "You don't know what a mother is. You were picked up out of a gutter where she left you. You're no good." I was stunned.

A year later my foster father died, and I started my search at the age of 17. I began at the office of vital statistics in Winnipeg, where I hoped to obtain a birth certificate, but there was no registration of my birth.

Later, through contacts made by an employer, I learned from the Director of Child Welfare in Winnipeg the names of two relatives.

Several years after that I made an attempt to secure more information. First I visited the Healthwin Hospital in Winnipeg, where I was born. Many hundreds, perhaps thousands, of people were born in this private maternity hospital when it was operated by the late Anna More, a nurse who died in 1937, but I have met only one other adopted person who was born there.

When I first saw this large, old house, by then a rooming house, I felt a little closer to my roots. This was my birthplace, where my birth mother and I had shared a space for a time before we went our separate ways.

Through old residents of the street I obtained the name of the retired postman who used to deliver mail to the house where I was born, and I contacted him for information as to where Mrs. More had gone. It turned out she had moved to the United States to live with her daughter, who informed me of her mother's death. Not knowing what else could be done, I packed away my search, temporarily.

The years after that were busy ones, with work to be done and babies to care for, and the search waited patiently in the back of my mind. But often, when seated on a bus or walking along a street, I would catch myself wondering, as my eyes scanned the faces of strangers, if one of them might be related to me.

Nothing more was done about this unfinished business until ten years later when, on moving back to Winnipeg after a sojourn in the United States, I called a physician who had practised at Healthwin at one time. His advice was to forget my quest. "Put it out of your mind," he said, "and concentrate on the future." I spoke to a social worker and he definitely knew I would never uncover the truth. The search was stored away once more, for a while.

This is the slow journey some of us must take. We move ahead while looking back over our shoulder for a glimmer of our beginnings. It's been called biological bewilderment. An adopted person described it as an attempt to make sense of a book when the first chapter is missing. Finding even a bit of those missing roots is a meaningful experience.

Always busy with husband, children and work, that need for roots remained "on hold" in the back of my mind, waiting until there was more time for searching. My conception of time was altered quite suddenly in 1970 in a car accident that took our only daughter's life shortly before her ninth birthday. Clearly there was no certain tomorrow. I must have known that before, and yet did not know, or gave it no thought. The years had gone by so quickly and already it might be too late to resolve my unfinished business.

A few years later, when energy was restored, the final search began. "Are you sure it's a good idea to turn over old stones?" a close friend wondered. If you turn over a stone beside a trail you will find bugs crawling about. Was that her image of my background? When the sun shines on a dark area it becomes warm and pleasant. I saw only the sun.

In less than a year of almost full-time searching I found my roots, although it took longer to identify and contact various people. It can be done. But it can be a lonely undertaking, with those closest to you hard pressed to understand your quest. The kindred spirits in a self-help group are the best support, for only another adopted person seems able to truly understand what it means to be ignorant of and separated from one's origins.

Joan Vanstone, national director of Parent Finders, spent nine years looking for her natural father, who had died by the time she was able to trace him. Gathering up her courage, she contacted his brother, her uncle, and was immediately glad of the decision. "Welcome to the family," he said, even though he had not known of her existence before.

Through her uncle, she was able to see pictures of her father, whose looks she has inherited, and to learn about his life. Her natural mother also had died by the time she was traced, but Joan was able to visit her mother's closest friend to see where her mother had lived and to hear about her life. "Even though my mother was dead, I was glad to have found her," she said. "I felt that I had finally found my way home."

Discovering that the people for whom you have searched a long time are dead, especially if they died during your search, is a disappointment. People who have had this experience say that despite that disappointment they are glad they searched, for at least they know who their natural parents are, something about them, and what happened to them. The emptiness of not knowing is filled with knowledge that is comforting.

The courage to search is born of a natural need. Rodney, for example, was born in Toronto but, because of circumstances in his family life he grew up in an orphanage in England, separated from his natural parents and two full brothers for sixteen years. Once he had made up his mind to find his family, it took but three hours of library research to locate his brother Michael in an overseas telephone directory, and they soon were deep in conversation by telephone. With his brother's help, Rodney found an aunt and uncle who are assisting in the search for his parents and other brother.

A search can proceed even more quickly than that, as Michelle discovered when she contacted the Department of Social Services in Nova Scotia for her background information. It turned out that her birth mother had written to the office four years earlier, asking for information about her child. The search was over and a reunion was arranged.

7

COPING WITH THE FACTS

a. YOU CAN STOP ANYTIME

Long before you succeed in finding biological relatives in
your search for roots, you will begin to pick up the threads
of information that belong to your ancestral tapestry.
Some of these threads will give you an idea of the tapestry
design as a whole, so that by the time you have enough
threads to locate people you already sense something about
them.

Friends and family often worry that what you find will
be unpleasant, or even shocking. They assume that you
won't know anything until the day you actually find your
parents and then, according to this view, it will be too late
to protect yourself. It does not hurt to think about the type
of situation that, for you, would be too unpleasant to
stomach. But in this day and age, with all the grim facts of
peace and war that are played out for us on television, it is
difficult to imagine a natural family situation that could not
be understood and accepted.

Still, it depends on the kind of person you are and how
you react to situations. When pressed to think along these
lines during my search, I finally decided that if I found my
natural parents were cold-blooded murders, that indeed
would be nasty and I would not like it at all. But, of course,
that was not the situation I found. The point is that you
ought to consider what you can handle comfortably. You
may, like me, feel deep down that no matter what you find,
you would rather know than not know. And you realize
from the start that something went wrong, that there
was some problem of serious proportion in the beginning,
or you would not be searching for your origins.

When all other arguments fail, people who are nervous about searching fall back on the mother who was 15 when she gave birth. This is supposed to be a dreadful circumstance. In some cultures girls marry at puberty. In our own pioneer days couples married young. That is one point. The other is that even if your birth mother was 15 at the time, she would be at least 35 when you find her and probably older. She, too, has matured.

For one birth mother, finding her daughter and knowing she was alive and well, allowed for the "melting away of the guilt and fear and pain of 17 years."

Whatever facts you seem to be heading for, as you pick up indications in your search, remember that *you* began the tracing process and you can stop it at any time, if you feel the need. Sensitivity to your needs and ability to cope with reality, and to those for whom you are searching, will be your soundest guides.

Rape and incest are realities that could upset you, as those who would protect all adopted people from the truth forever, insist. If you are not squeamish, you may prefer the whole truth, but end your search without attempting reunion when you have reason to feel that it would be too painful for your original mother.

Sorosky, Baran and Pannor, in their book, *The Adoption Triangle*, referred to the professional argument that sordid origins are too destructive to be revealed to adoptees, a theory they claim was disputed by an experience shared with the authors by a social worker. It told of a middle-aged man who learned that he was born of an incestuous relationship between his mother, then a young girl, and her father, his grandfather. The social worker reported that he accepted this information well, but chose not to attempt a reunion with his mother because of the pain it might bring to her. He felt, however, that he had achieved adulthood as a result of his search, and could accept himself as a whole person.

b. WHAT YOU SEE IS WHAT YOU GET

Real people have flaws, problems, quirks and individual personalities, no matter what their station in life. Some people are warm and able to establish instant rapport with a person they have just met, while others are more cautious or reserved. Some people are easily disappointed; some are plainly disappointing. But whatever they are, real people are not fantasy people.

In the summer of 1977, Susan Slade, 22, went to Guelph, Ontario for a reunion visit with her younger sister, Francine, and afterward was interviewed by the *Winnipeg Tribune.* The sisters had been separated in childhood when they were adopted by different families in Ontario. Slade, who ended up married in Winnipeg, was quoted as saying that she had hoped her sister would be "rich, popular and skinny as anything. I wanted her to be all those things, something I wasn't."

Instead, she found another human being like herself and was disappointed. Both girls felt unloved. Both were fat.

"Maybe I should have let well enough alone," she said. "You think they are going to love you more than the other ones do. It's a feeling of wanting to belong to someone. I thought it would be automatic embraces, stars and everything." And finally, "She's my sister and she's not supposed to be like that." Slade could have benefited from counselling and the experiences of others in a group to prepare her for a more realistic reunion.

c. TWO SETS OF PARENTS

One thing adopted people can't change is the fact that they have two sets of parents: two mothers and two fathers. Each pair has a different meaning for you. The meaning of your original parents actually becomes clearer once you know who they are, what they are like, what they do and

57

think: when they become real to you. Your second parents (or third, or whoever you grew up with) are the parents you know intimately, and whose life is part of your life.

Adopted people who have completed a search do not seem to have problems sorting everyone out, usually continuing to call their adoptive mother "Mom" and their first mother by her given name.

The problem seems greater for non-adopted people. Some go so far as to insist that the fact of adoption ought never to be revealed because of this, which would be the ultimate in fraud and abuse of human rights.

In a search you are looking for answers to important questions and for a sense of continuity that is missing in your life. You may want to see a face in which you see yourself mirrored and to know your biological history.

In *Beyond The Best Interests of the Child* (Joseph Goldstein, Anna Freud, Albert J. Solnit), the everyday, caring, nurturing parents are described as "psychological parents" whether biological or surrogate, and the authors dismiss the importance of blood ties for anyone. Your emotional attachments to psychological parents are not going to be wiped out by finding your roots as an adult. For one thing, your original parents likely live separate lives and you will have to find them separately and see them separately. This is a point that adoptive parents tend to forget when they become alarmed about searching and envision "their children" running back to original parents.

Some adopted people do discover that their original parents married each other after relinquishing their child for adoption. This is what Ann Reed of Victoria, British Columbia found when she searched for roots. Her original parents married six months after they gave her up. She described what it was like to find and visit them and four brothers and sisters in an interview published in *Monday Magazine* in the fall of 1977. After the visit they began to exchange letters and she began to develop perspective following a time of information and emotional overload.

"When I first got home I really resented my own (adoptive) parents — which is ridiculous!" Reed was quoted as saying. "Then suddenly — it was like an enlightenment — I thought — these people really are my parents, and they love me and I love them — and I've since felt closer to them than I ever have before. And this gives me rein to deal with the other family. I've got them both in perspective."

In the fall of 1976, a British woman who was put up for adoption at the age of three months in 1944, was reunited with her natural parents, Joseph and Dorothy Gerrior, of Collingwood, Ontario. The *Canadian Press* reported that Janice Fudge discovered her adoption only in 1972 and subsequently searched for her parents. "My parents were absolutely overjoyed when I wrote to them," she said. The Gerriors met in Britain during World War II. Gerrior was already married when Janice was born and it was decided to put her up for adoption. Father eventually was divorced and married Janice's mother, but then it was too late to get their daughter back. "Being reunited with Janice is just like a million dollars to us," Gerrior said, after Mrs. Fudge was flown to Canada for the reunion by the *Sunday Mirror*, a British newspaper.

8
REUNION

a. FACE TO FACE

Whether to attempt a reunion and reconciliation with members of one's family is a very personal matter and a decision depends, in part, on the wishes of the people who are found. Some adopted people choose to end their search with the information obtained and are satisfied. Others have a deep need to see blood relatives, face to face, at least once.

Such a meeting is an emotional, exhausting, moving and joyous occasion, especially when meeting a parent for the first time. Soon after contacting my mother I wrote to her asking for an opportunity to meet her. She agreed, and in further correspondence we completed the arrangements for our visit, which entailed an overseas trip for me. I had given my reasons for wanting to see her, which she understood, and she too wanted to see me but was unable to travel.

On the plane bound for England I began to wonder what I, a middle-aged woman, was doing, on the verge of visiting an elderly stranger who was also my mother. There was no question in my mind that I wanted to see her — had to see her — but at that moment I was bound to feel a little nervous, as she too did. How would it go? Would we be able to talk as friends? "What do you want to talk about?" she had asked. "I come with no recriminations," I replied.

Airborne, I began to plan alternate activities for my time overseas, just in case the visit was brief. It was a relief to find a welcoming letter from my mother waiting for me at the hotel in London.

A few days later I was in a small, seaside hotel, on the top floor, preparing for our initial meeting. We had arranged that I would meet my mother in the downstairs lobby to save her climbing the staircase, as the hotel had no elevator. But, suddenly, there was a light knock on my door and I opened it to see my slight, smiling mother who had arrived early and was anxious to see how her baby had turned out, her smile covering inner anxiety over this unbelievable moment.

She had been told, so long ago, that she was not to ever try to find me, and as she said over and over, she had to promise and keep her word, and sign papers, and she could not think how I had managed to find her. "But I made no promises," I said. We sat down to talk.

"I hope you like music," she said, right off, "because you should."

My father and uncles were music lovers and had sung in choirs for most of their lives, she said. This touched a chord deep within me, for I had sung in school choirs from my earliest grades and Manitoba's spring Musical Festival was for me the highlight of the year. We talked easily of these things, as if picking up a conversation broken off earlier, exchanged gifts, and I got out my little purse album to show off the pictures I had brought of my husband and children. Then she was telling me her life story and her poignant memories of my beginning. Later we went down for tea and more talk and when we parted it was with an invitation for me to have tea next day at her home, which she shared with another widow to whom I was introduced as a friend.

In my spare time there I wandered about the town looking at sights and visiting shops or took short bus trips to other towns. Gradually I began to feel tall enough. All my life, living with tall people, I had felt my five-foot height abnormally short. Urged to eat more, to stand straight, to be more like the people around me, I was convinced that tall was better. Now all around me I saw short people looking quite satisfied to be the way they were, and I began to feel normal. Shortness was part of my heritage. A sense of continuity crept over me comfortably.

My mother and I went through her pictures and I was invited to choose whatever I wished to take home for my album. I saw the resemblance between us in pictures of her youth but it was my father I looked like, she said.

I did not know then it would take another year of hard work to find him and obtain my paternal family history, which he did share with me. In the meantime, the week of visiting passed quickly. I have always found it hard to visit for long in anyone's home and in this case I was especially relieved to be staying at a hotel, to which I could retreat at night to mull over the day's happenings. I believe it was good for my mother as well, and that in general first visits should not be overwhelming with constant togetherness.

As it was, my head was filled with family lore that would take a while to sift through and be absorbed with familiarity, and I had not felt so emotional in years. I had been anxious to meet my brother on this visit, but my mother was not ready for that and, reluctantly, I put the wish aside for the time. But siblings are important, representing perhaps the present and future, and because the pain of relinquishment is not involved, good relationships can develop more easily.

On our last evening my mother took me out to dinner, wearing the corsage I gave her. She was glad I had come, although she admitted to having had misgivings when the visit was first suggested. "Maybe we'll meet again," she said. I certainly hoped so.

Next morning, as the train moved slowly past her house in a fine rain, she stood on the porch waving a white cloth in farewell. A lump rose in my throat and the dammed up tears poured out. I had carried a deep sense of loss for long years. I was afraid I would never see her again, because of distance and her age if for no other reason. But by some miracle or destiny we had met and we felt good about each other. Since then we have come to know one another better, and my life has been enriched and normalized through contact with brothers, sisters and other relatives, and the knowledge of our heritage.

b. SENSITIVITY IS A TWO-WAY STREET

I have heard dozens and dozens of reunion stories and not once have any of them involved an adopted person turning up suddenly, uninvited, on anyone's doorstep. This is the popular conception of reunion, but it does not usually take place that way, nor is it advised by adoptee groups.

I did read of an adopted person who simply arrived, unannounced, knowing that her parents had married after she was given up, and fortunately she was welcomed. But most of the time, adopted people are too sensitive, too aware of the risk of rejection, too aware of the emotional nature of reunion for all parties, to intrude without prior arrangement.

This kind of sensitivity has to work both ways, however, and original parents who actually believe that all parental obligations and responsibilities can be completely removed by the signing of a piece of paper, and would therefore deny their offspring's need of information or a meeting, do not reveal much sensitivity. It is an irresponsible attitude that is encouraged by the signing of papers during relinquishment, which could very easily include a statement to cover future need of information, despite relinquishment of parental child-rearing obligations and responsibilities.

Take the time to request and arrange your reunion with care, remembering that while you have had ample time to prepare yourself, the relative you wish to see may be unprepared. Some people find it useful to have an intermediary request the reunion visit.

Recently, a searcher located her original mother and soon after was thrilled to find her brother. When she spoke to him by telephone for the first time he was delighted and expressed keen interest in meeting her and their mother. As it happened, however, he was about to be married to a widow with two children but he thought he could arrange a meeting with the sister and mother within a few weeks.

Everyone was in high spirits at the prospect of being reunited. Weeks went by, but the sister and mother did not hear from him again. Months passed with no word. Disappointed, they came to the conclusion that he did not wish to meet them and, respecting his wishes, they did not try to contact him either.

Then, nine months after he was first called, the man arrived at his sister's house unexpectedly with his wife and children, explaining that so much had been happening in his life all of a sudden when the sister called that he had had to take his time about the reunion. By then he had adjusted to his marriage and felt ready to see, for the first time, a sister and mother he had never expected to meet.

This need for time is important to remember, because the people you contact in a search do have their own busy lives, usually, and you have no way of knowing what else is going on for them at the moment of contact. Give them time and, if they are interested, a meeting will come about.

c. WHAT ARE YOU UP TO?

Sometimes motivation is questioned, even in the midst of pleasure. Why does my grown offspring want to see me, a mother may wonder and, sometimes ask. What is the reason?

A mother who was laughing and crying happily when called by an intermediary suddenly asked: "I wonder what he wants? Oh, I didn't mean it that way. I just wondered." One can speculate about what she meant. The intermediary merely explained that the son did not want anything more than to see his mother, a blood relative, to restore the broken link. It was up to her. "Of course I want to see him," the mother said.

The question about motivation came up one evening when I was asked to speak to a group of prospective adopting parents. "Do you think they might want revenge?" a man asked. I have never met anyone, or heard of anyone, searching with that motive, although anything is possible in human relations — any human relations: marriage, divorce, parenthood, and so on.

Parent Finders in Canada has records of 600 reunions, and there have been others reported in newspapers and some unreported no doubt. No one has heard that anger or a revenge motive has been a factor in any of these reunions. But I have heard of adopted adults who, on being contacted for reunion with searching natural parents, have refused any contact or communication. From this I have concluded that the adoptee who has been deeply wounded by the separation from original family, and who may still be very angry about it, does not search at all.

Adopted people and first parents who face such rejection bear up better than you might imagine. They know from the start of their search that this is a possibility. It is heartbreaking, and they are sad when the broken link can't be mended, but after a while they say much the same thing: "At least I know. Knowing is better than going around wondering."

A warm, motherly woman found her son living in Edmonton, but when he was contacted this man not only refused to meet his mother, even once, he sent her a letter through a third party saying he did not ever wish to speak to her or see her. Stung, his mother went to Edmonton to have a look at this young man born to her more than 20 years earlier, whose nature seemed so different from her own. She could not understand his reaction. She respected his wishes, however, and after seeing for herself that he had grown tall and handsome and looked very well, she went home and has not tried to contact him again. The hurt is there, but as she says, "At least I know he's alive and well."

It might help mothers who long to see their relinquished offspring to remember that adopted people generally begin active searching only in maturity, anywhere from the mid-twenties on.

It can happen that the found one is pleased, but a new problem appears when a spouse is annoyed or jealous. An engaging young woman found her twin sister and together they traced their first mother. The mother was called and, when she grasped the situation, she went silent. "But Mother, didn't you want us to find you?" her daughter asked. Yes, she did, she did, the mother said, finding her tongue, but she was not sure how her husband would take the news. She promised to return the call when she had the problem worked out. The mother decided to explain everything right away to her husband and he gave his wife "permission" to have contact with her twin daughters but insisted they were never to step inside his door.

A reunion dinner was arranged at a restaurant. The night of the meeting the mother's husband also turned up and, after seeing and having an opportunity to talk with the daughters, he changed his attitude completely. They were not only welcome in "his" house, but he liked them. They visit, but home is still with their adoptive parents, who shared in the search.

Reunions are something like the institution of marriage. Both require tact, give and take, patience and love. It took a year before a hostile wife, with brothers and sisters of her own, could concede that her husband had a right to enjoy having the friendship of a newly found sister. Give these things time to work themselves out.

Adopted people must be allowed this experience in their maturity, as much as they are allowed to venture into a marriage that may or may not be successful. At an adoption conference in Seattle, a man who introduced himself as "an adoptee first, then a dentist," stated the matter this way: "I want the state to get out of my life. I needed protection when I was a child but now I'm grown up, thank you very much. The only two things sealed I know of are the Warren Report and my birth record." He was not pleased by either secret.

Dr. Ruth B. Weeks, assistant professor of psychiatry at the University of Virginia, has said, "Continued contact between the biological parents and the adoptee during the childhood and adolescent period can be growth-promoting for both the biological parents and the adoptee and would circumvent the fantasies and doubts the adoptee has about his inherent worth."

It would help alleviate any guilt feelings the biological parent has for abandoning the child, she added. While such early contact would be a challenge to both the adoptive and biological parents and might be a potential source of conflict she said it would be better than today's existing adoption practices.

Dr. Weeks studied 30 adopted adults and concluded that overall they were "bright, skilled, and self-demanding. They were sensitive and attractive personalities, yet somewhat difficult to deal with and somewhat impatient with conventional demands and roles."

The relationship between the adoptee and family correlated positively with the adoptive parents' feelings about the biological parents. More than half the adoptees who had good relationships with the adoptive family, she said, felt either positively or neutrally about their biological parents. The small percentage who had poor family relationships felt their biological parents were looked down on, or were disapproved of, by the adoptive parents.

Punitive attitudes to biological parents do come through in letters to newspapers from some adopting parents. An adoptive mother in Chilliwack, British Columbia put it this way: "Her natural mother had to give her up at birth. I'm sorry for her for that, but somewhere a price must be paid." There is an assumption of sin where there may have been none, especially as definitions of sin vary.

9

GENEALOGY

"How hard a matter it is to sifte out ye truth in these matters of Genealogye."

— *Sir William Dugdale, 1651*

a. AFTER THE SEARCH

When the search is over and your files are bulging with information about your roots, you may feel for a while like a traveller at the end of a long journey. It can take a few days after a trip to unpack and get over the feeling of constant movement, as if there must be yet another train or plane to board, something else to come.

That type of restlessness, even depression for some, is natural in the fourth stage of search, regardless of whether you feel satisfied with the outcome or had difficulty obtaining needed knowledge. You have expended a great deal of time and concentration on your search, and perhaps felt the exhilaration of contact and reunion, and now you have to simmer down into a more usual routine. There is no telling how long it will take to unwind from searching; a lot depends on you and what else is happening in your life.

It is especially important for you to have a post-search activity in mind. By collecting available pictures, organizing your notes, and preparing your history, you put the jigsaw pieces of your search together in an orderly way with a sense of completion. When it all comes together and makes sense, you can turn your attention to the future part of your life story. If, as a result of your search for roots, your future includes some new biological relationships, so much the better.

b. FAR SPREADING ROOTS

Adopted people who begin their search with the idea of tracing only their original parents often end up hearing about or finding other relatives or long dead ancestors. Your spreading roots include grandparents, great-grandparents, brothers, sisters, aunts, uncles, stories of immigration, and other lore.

Tracing roots is a fascinating and unpredictable process for anyone who becomes interested in genealogy. Nobody knows what will turn up next or how far the trail will lead before it turns cold.

The trail could lead back to nobility or serfs. It could turn up an ancestral scoundrel, a will making provision for an illegitimate child some generations back, or a connection with one of the Fathers of Confederation. That is part of the fun of genealogical research for most people.

My genealogical research produced a great-great-grandfather who was born in the 18th century and became a weaver. There were Quakers in my background who preached at their peril in times of religious persecution; stonemasons; writers; teachers; farmers: a whole variety of people, as in any family history. Learning about them gave me a better feeling about myself.

Relatives have been generous, often sending me the only copy of an old photograph so that I could have a print made for my records. You too may have collected some pictures which, together with other information, have strengthened your feeling of being rooted. The task now is to put all this information together in an orderly way, in a package that gives you a sense of completion.

c. CHARTING YOUR ROOTS

Your library will have books on genealogy and how to prepare a pedigree chart (see Sample #1 and #1A) with a standard method for the listing of entries. You can prepare

SAMPLE #1
PEDIGREE CHART
(with instructions)

PEDIGREE CHART

NO. 1 ON THIS CHART IS

THE SAME PERSON AS NO. _____

ON CHART NO. _____

8 YOUR GREAT GRANDFATHER
BORN
WHERE _____
MARRIED
WHERE
DIED
WHERE

4 YOUR FATHER'S FATHER
BORN (your grandfather)
WHERE
MARRIED
WHERE
DIED
WHERE

9 YOUR GREAT GRANDMOTHER
BORN
WHERE _____
DIED
WHERE

2 YOUR FATHER
BORN
WHERE
MARRIED
WHERE
DIED
WHERE

10 YOUR GREAT GRANDFATHER
BORN
WHERE _____
MARRIED
WHERE
DIED
WHERE

5 YOUR FATHER'S MOTHER
BORN (your grandmother)
WHERE
DIED
WHERE

11 YOUR GREAT GRANDMOTHER
BORN
WHERE _____
DIED
WHERE

1 YOUR NAME
BORN
WHERE
MARRIED
WHERE
DIED
WHERE

YOUR SPOUSE
NAME OF HUSBAND OR WIFE

12 YOUR GREAT GRANDFATHER
BORN
WHERE _____
MARRIED
WHERE
DIED
WHERE

6 YOUR MOTHER'S FATHER
BORN (your grandfather)
WHERE
MARRIED
WHERE
DIED
WHERE

13 YOUR GREAT GRANDMOTHER
BORN
WHERE _____
DIED
WHERE

3 YOUR MOTHER
BORN
WHERE
DIED
WHERE

14 YOUR GREAT GRANDFATHER
BORN
WHERE _____
MARRIED
WHERE
DIED
WHERE

7 YOUR MOTHER'S MOTHER
BORN (your grandmother)
WHERE
DIED
WHERE

15 YOUR GREAT GRANDMOTHER
BORN
WHERE _____
DIED
WHERE

ORDER OF DATA
NAME: John Henry BROWN
PLACE: Bramley, Hampshire, England
DATE: 2 September, 1832

SAMLE #1A
PEDIGREE CHART
(completed)

PEDIGREE CHART

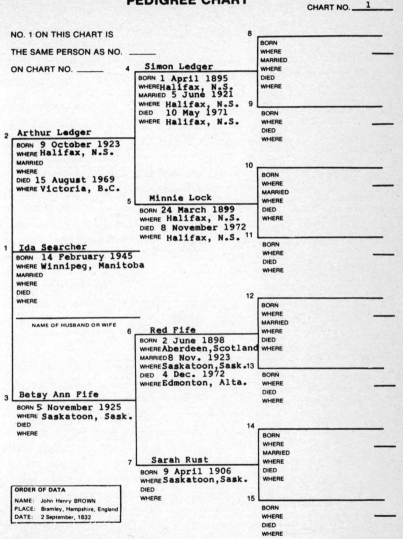

NO. 1 ON THIS CHART IS

THE SAME PERSON AS NO. ____

ON CHART NO. ____

8

BORN
WHERE
MARRIED
WHERE
DIED
WHERE

4 Simon Ledger
BORN 1 April 1895
WHERE Halifax, N.S.
MARRIED 5 June 1921
WHERE Halifax, N.S.
DIED 10 May 1971
WHERE Halifax, N.S.

9
BORN
WHERE
DIED
WHERE

2 Arthur Ledger
BORN 9 October 1923
WHERE Halifax, N.S.
MARRIED
WHERE
DIED 15 August 1969
WHERE Victoria, B.C.

10
BORN
WHERE
MARRIED
WHERE
DIED
WHERE

5 Minnie Lock
BORN 24 March 1899
WHERE Halifax, N.S.
DIED 8 November 1972
WHERE Halifax, N.S.

11
BORN
WHERE
DIED
WHERE

1 Ida Searcher
BORN 14 February 1945
WHERE Winnipeg, Manitoba
MARRIED
WHERE
DIED
WHERE

NAME OF HUSBAND OR WIFE

12
BORN
WHERE
MARRIED
WHERE
DIED
WHERE

6 Red Fife
BORN 2 June 1898
WHERE Aberdeen, Scotland
MARRIED 8 Nov. 1923
WHERE Saskatoon, Sask.
DIED 4 Dec. 1972
WHERE Edmonton, Alta.

13
BORN
WHERE
DIED
WHERE

3 Betsy Ann Fife
BORN 5 November 1925
WHERE Saskatoon, Sask.
DIED
WHERE

14
BORN
WHERE
MARRIED
WHERE
DIED
WHERE

7 Sarah Rust
BORN 9 April 1906
WHERE Saskatoon, Sask.
DIED
WHERE

15
BORN
WHERE
DIED
WHERE

ORDER OF DATA
NAME: John Henry BROWN
PLACE: Bramley, Hampshire, England
DATE: 2 September, 1832

71

a genealogy chart on a large sheet of paper or purchase blueprint paper from a print shop for this purpose. Your main chart can be cross-referenced to individual charts for family groups, and the information for those charts can be recorded initially on family record sheets. (See Sample #2 and #2A.) All of these aids are available wherever supplies for genealogists are sold, including the Genealogical Library of the Church of Jesus Christ of Latter Day Saints.

I began recording my roots on family record sheets purchased at the church library. The sheets are inexpensive and are punched ready for insertion in a three-ring binder. You can buy the special family record binder available at the library or use any three-ring binder, as I did. The record sheets are invaluable in sorting out who is who as names accumulate. You can see at a glance, as you go along, who was born when and where, dates of death and marriage, and your sources of information.

Enter names in full, printing or typing the surname in capitals. When entering dates, put the day before the month as professional genealogists do. Working from your family record sheets, you will find it easier to transfer data to your large genealogy chart, where of course you probably will have to draw some extra lines to connect your name with those of your original parents, unless your parents were married to each other.

d. WRITING YOUR FAMILY HISTORY

Everyone can write, unless illiterate. If you can write a note for the milkman or letters to friends, you can write your history. Start with yourself, working back to your ancestors or begin with the earliest known ancestor putting down everything you have learned about this person. Do the same for later ancestors, writing about where they came from if they were born in another land, and what they did for a living. If they emigrated to North America you may pick up some interesting tales about their early years as they struggled to settle in a new

SAMPLE #2
FAMILY GROUP RECORD

FAMILY GROUP RECORD

HUSBAND	Red Fife			Occupation	Farmer
Born	2 June 1898		Place	Aberdeen, Scotland	
Chr.			Place		
Marr.	8 November 1923		Place	Saskatoon, Saskatchewan	
Died	4 December 1972		Place	Edmonton, Alberta	
Bur.	7 December 1972		Place	Saskatoon, Saskatchewan	
Father	Patrick Scoot			Mother	Martha Berry
Other Wives					

WIFE	Sarah Rust				
Born	9 April 1906		Place	Saskatoon, Saskatchewan	
Chr.			Place		
Died			Place		
Bur.			Place		
Father	Toban Willow			Mother	Matilda Ash
Other Husbands					

	Children	Sex	When Born / When Died	Where Born / Where Died	Marriage Date & Place / To Whom
1	Patrick Toban	M	1 Nov 1924	Saskatoon, Sask.	3 June 1947 Calgary / Joan Lively
2	Betsy Ann	F	5 Nov 1925	Saskatoon, Sask.	4 July 1951 Toronto / Don Mills
3	William Red	M	1 Jan 1926 / 8 Aug 1926	Saskatoon, Sask. / Saskatoon, Sask.	
4	Thomas	M	5 May 1927 / 9 Oct 1974	Saskatoon, Sask. / Calgary, Alta.	
5	James Ash	M	4 1929	Saskatoon, Sask.	6 Dec 1958 Calgary / Mary Foothill
6					
7					
8					
9					
10					
11					
12					
13					
14					
15					

Sources of Information	Other Marriages
Saskatchewan Directories	
Obituary of Red Fife	
Patrick and James Fife	

ORDER OF DATA

NAME: John Henry BROWN
PLACE: Bramley, Hampshire, England
DATE: 2 September, 1832

SAMPLE #2A
FAMILY GROUP RECORD

FAMILY GROUP RECORD

HUSBAND FATHER	Arthur Ledger		Occupation Accountant	
Born 9 October 1923		Place	Halifax, Nova Scotia	
Chr.		Place		
Marr.		Place		
Died 15 August 1969		Place	Victoria, British Columbia	
Bur. 18 August 1969		Place	Victoria, British Columbia	
Father Simon Ledger			Mother Minnie Lock	
Other Wives				

WIFE MOTHER	Betsy Ann Fife			
Born 5 November 1925		Place	Saskatoon, Saskatchewan	
Chr.		Place		
Died		Place		
Bur.		Place		
Father Red Fife			Mother Sarah Rust	
Other Husbands				

	Children	Sex	When Born / When Died	Where Born / Where Died	Marriage Date & Place / To Whom
1	Ida Searcher	F	14 Feb 1945	Winnipeg, Man.	
2					
3					
4					
5					
6					
7					
8					
9					
10					
11					
12					
13					
14					
15					

Sources of Information	Other Marriages
Marriage Record of Betsy Ann Fife & Don Mills	
Death Certificate of Arthur Ledger	
Verbal Confirmation of Betsy Ann Mills	

ORDER OF DATA

NAME: John Henry BROWN
PLACE: Bramley, Hampshire, England
DATE: 2 September, 1832

All forms courtesy of Graham Edis, co-author with Shirley Edis of Trace Your Family Tree *workbook (Toronto: McGraw-Hill Ryerson Limited, 1977).*

country. Perhaps the family name was spelled in a different way originally and was changed by someone in the Department of Immigration who could not spell the first way, thus complicating your search.

Your parents and other relatives also will have stories to tell you, if you can get on that footing with them. Usually people are ready to share family history, unless it is a history they would rather not remember. And usually, again, that attitude comes from the family member who has had a rough time. Others might well have a different view of family history.

When you have the ancestors settled and "written up," write a brief sketch about each person you have come to know in your families of origin. If one of them is an interesting character, so much the better. It will make good reading for your children and theirs.

Start your own story with where and when you were born, your separation and your adoption, or whatever the outcome was following the separation. It's your story and each story is a little different. Adoption may have been preceded by a stay in an orphanage or in foster homes, or you may never have been adopted at all but lived with foster parents. One searcher learned that her father died before she was born and soon afterward her mother became ill with tuberculosis and could not look after her child. So, even though she had been born to a married couple, circumstances intervened and she was placed in an orphanage as an infant, living there for three years. Then, unable to earn enough money to pay for her daughter's care, the mother signed a consent for adoption. This adopted person's children and grandchildren may count their blessings when they read about her start in life, a beginning she did not know about before doing her search.

At this point you could continue your life history with a section on your adoptive family and your life with them: school days, marriage, children and so on. Include any pictures you have been able to obtain, or assemble them in a multiple picture frame that can be purchased in a variety of sizes.

Writing a history can be fun; it can serve as a bridge between a period of intense search activity and getting back to your usual way of life; and it is a concrete result of all your work. By the time it is done you will be ready to turn your attention to other activities and some of those new relationships you are developing may be gelling nicely.

10

WHAT ABOUT THE FUTURE?

a. CHANGING ATTITUDES

The subject of adoption is being treated with a candor today that would have been impossible five years ago. Theories and practices are in question and the concerns of adopted people are being considered in a way that is encouraging.

Social service workers and officials who once regarded questioning adoptees as emotionally disturbed have changed their minds and now recognize the need to know as a normal development for a person severed from roots. It is not a unanimous change of mind by any means, but a significant change in point of view has taken place.

Less than two years ago, the influential Child Welfare League of America reaffirmed the principle of confidentiality in adoption, *but* advised social agencies that firm assurances could no longer be made regarding disclosure of information to adult adoptees.

Other cracks in the wall of silence have appeared.

In 1976, the Ontario Committee on Record Disclosure, set up by the provincial government, recommended that Ontario adopt the reunion registry concept, with a mediation board to handle special cases. In 1978, after a long and often heated debate, Ontario legislators passed, by a narrow 37-36 vote, a bill for establishment of a three-party disclosure registry. The legislation gives adopting parents power of veto over disclosure, but it is a step forward. Some proviso is expected in handling the consent of adopting parents in cases where they are elderly or infirm. Adult adoptees, who are free to make their own decisions in other areas of life, are not likely to be satisfied with any consent apron strings attached to this type of legislation; nor are birth parents who wish to experience the healing of reunion contact. Nevertheless, the Ontario legislation is a hard-won breakthrough.

Comprehensive studies on disclosure have been carried out in Alberta and Saskatchewan, where policies have been prepared in readiness for implementation at some point in time; and adoption legislation, policies and procedures have been reviewed in British Columbia.

"While governments stonewall and stand still on adoption record disclosure, it is becoming clear that no policy is itself a policy," said David A. Cruickshank, a law professor at the University of Calgary.

Noting that governments are assigning to courts and administrators the decisions on record disclosure, reunion counselling and adoption reunions, he predicts conflicting case-by-case decisions by executive and judicial branches that will add to the costs, "frustrations and injustices sadly familiar in the family law field."

"Forging and expressing new shifts in social policy is the job of legislatures," Cruickshank concludes. "Let's get on with it."

b. OPEN RECORDS STAND

The Sixth North American Conference on Adoptable Children recommended in 1978 that the following be implemented by state legislation:

> All information in original birth records shall be available on request at age 18 to persons who were adopted;
>
> All information from original birth records shall be available to birth parents at any time on request;
>
> All information to be made available at age 18 to the adult person who was adopted pertaining to medical, sociological, physiological and genetic history as included in court and agency records on request up to and including all identifying names;
>
> All information to be made available to birth parents concerning court, agency or other records pertaining to

offspring who have reached the age of majority, 18; up to
and including all identifying names.

This is a significant step by a conference that was
sponsored by the North American Council on Adoptable
Children, the School of Social Work, University of
Washington, and the Interracial Family Association of
Seattle, with conference faculty drawn from university
faculties, agency executives, and judicial circles.

Registrants included social workers, adoptive parents,
birth parents and adopted people from the United States
and Canada.

It was clear that a number of things were responsible for
the receptivity to changing legislation and attitudes: the
shortage of children available for adoption under present
legislation; the increasing numbers of children in foster
care who need greater stability; economics; and the
growing demand of birth parents and adopted people to
have their needs considered.

The foster home population in the United States has
grown to such proportions that it equals the population of
San Francisco, a city with 652 200 residents. (No
comparison is available for Canada.)

At the same time the continent is short of children for
adoption and many childless couples pin their hopes on
international adoption. Foster care has become a new route
to adoption, but certain changes are needed to make this
more generally possible.

"Adoption nationally is changing to an open system,"
said Sanford N. Katz, professor of law at Boston College
Law School. "Open adoption may be a reality within five to
ten years."

This could help reduce the foster care population, he
explained. Many foster children have had some kind of
continuing connection with original family and this
connection cannot be severed. Open adoption would
involve a wider family, including birth parents and
grandparents, rather than exclusivity with adoptive
families. Termination agreements, through which birth

parents terminate parental responsibilities under state laws, "have been a hindrance" to adoption in foster care situations, said Dr. Katz, who has been involved in drafting model legislation for a new type of adoption for the U.S. federal Health, Education and Welfare Department in Washington, D.C.

Another problem mentioned was that some foster parents would be ready to adopt the child or children in their care except for the problem of inheritance rights. They often prefer to confine their estate to their grown born children.

"Adoption is not always the answer," Dr. Katz said, "but guardianship is needed to give permanency to foster care without breaking the tie with natural parents. Older kids have some attachment to birth parents who come in and out of their lives, but they can deal with foster parent guardians on a permanent basis. It is workable."

So far courts in the United States have found no constitutional rights for opening records, "yet legislators are moving in a different direction . . . to make some change in adoption laws." A new terminology is being developed to replace traditional words such as "adoption," and some thought has been given to "managing conservator" as a term to describe the permanent guardian.

c. SOME EXAMPLES OF CHANGING LEGISLATION

There is a growing tendency in state legislatures in the U.S. to move toward opening up adoption records. Connecticut passed a complex act in 1977 to provide for the gathering and releasing of information relating to adoptions. Only Alabama now allows access to both the original birth certificate and the court decrees. Original birth certificates only are available to adult adoptees in Kansas and Florida, while Virginia and South Dakota statutes limit inspection by an adult adoptee to the relevant court records.

In California, a bill to provide for a reunion registry had passed both chambers of the state legislature at the time of writing, but was likely to be modified in order to receive the governor's support.

Minnesota enacted a new disclosure law, effective June, 1977, that is not acceptable to many adoptee activist groups. The decision of disclosure lies with the original parents, if they can be found, of people, 21 years old or older, adopted before August, 1977. Written requests for disclosure are submitted to the State Registrar of Vital Statistics, who forwards requests to the welfare department which has six months in which to locate the petitioner's natural parents. If the adoption was finalized before August, 1977, no information will be disclosed if either parent objects. If they are deceased or can't be found, a court order must be obtained to get the information.

In Illinois, a group called Yesterday's Children is challenging the sealed records provisions of state legislation, alleging that the statutes deny the right to receive information as protected by the First Amendment and also that they infringe on the adoptee's privacy rights.

An adoption registry in which natural parents can file their consent for disclosure of information is included in a proposed bill being prepared for introduction to the Washington state legislature early in 1979. The draft bill provides for an adopted person 18 years or over to receive such information from the adoption registry if there is consent.

Currently, an adoptee's access to records in Washington depends on the interpretation of a statute which states that the records of the registrar are secret unless otherwise provided by the court. The records may be disclosed only by order of the court for "good cause."

Under the proposed legislation, consent by either parent would be sufficient to allow disclosure.

The bill and discussion by professionals and adoptive parents from all over the United States, parts of Canada, New Zealand and Australia at the adoption conference in Seattle, centred around the mechanics of achieving open records. The merits and justice of such a policy had been resolved earlier.

"Perhaps society has been too prone to feel the adoptive family can be a duplicate," said Charlotte De Armond, director of public relations for the Children's Home Society of California. "The fact is the child came from biological families and they are there."

In 1975, 3 000 adopted adults returned to Child Welfare League of America member agencies for information about their natural parents, and 1 500 natural parents returned seeking information or reunion with their relinquished children, now grown. The board of directors of the California Society has endorsed the reunion concept.

The state intervened by law many years ago, before it was known that adoptees would have a need for information, Ms. De Armond said, "so we are talking about withdrawing intervention" rather than creating new laws. She prepared a comprehensive booklet on *The Changing Face of Adoption* for the California society in the spring of 1976.

d. A FINAL COMMENT

There is not doubt that in future the law and the public will recognize that total severance of the adopted person from biological origins is cruel and unjust. All parties to adoption need to adjust to a new concept of this created relationship. Margaret Mead, the late anthropologist, psychologist, writer and teacher, expressed the challenge this way: "Surely if a young adult who has grown up with love has the strength to accept the reality of her beginnings, her birth parents and adoptive parents can do so as well!"

The *Medical Post* editorialized on October 10, 1978 in favor of disclosure of birth records and referred to studies done at the Children's Aid Society in Toronto. These showed "that many reunions can be most rewarding for all concerned." The secret, the editorial continued, appeared to be in preparation. "If birth mother and child are brought together slowly with exchange of letters and photographs the reunion seems to have a much better chance of success than when the reunion is totally unexpected."

The dialogue has begun. Mythology, secrecy and fear are being swept away by facts born of research and the clearly expressed needs of the people most affected by adoption.

If you wish to help bring about change, meet with or write your elected provincial representatives. For until more legislators are prepared to vote to amend restrictive legislation and guarantee on adoption that the adult adopted person will have access to birth information, including names, you will have to rely on your wits and courage to search out your origins.

APPENDIX 1

PROVINCIAL GOVERNMENT RESOURCES

Each province in Canada has its own policies regarding the kind of information that is available to enquiring adopted adults. The following information was supplied for this guide in the fall of 1978.

1. Alberta

The Department of Social Services and Community Health in Alberta makes available, on written request, both a standardized background information sheet with non-identifying information and a copy of the adoption order. It takes about a month to obtain this information. Identifying information is not available.

In reply to a question regarding a change in policy, Donald Alexander, Program Administrator, Adoption Programs, stated: "The 'reunion concept' is new to adoption. In part it means that all three parties to an adoption must take a broader understanding position than they have in the past. Such a change is a social one and I am confident that increasing openness by these parties will facilitate policy changes. The responsibility of a policy change for future adoptions is much easier than a policy which must deal with past events."

Direct enquiries for non-identifying background information is:

Mr. Donald Alexander, Program Administrator
Adoption Programs
Department of Social Services & Community Health
Seventh Street Plaza
10030 - 107th Street
Edmonton, Alberta
T5J 3E4

For a copy of your adoption order write to Mr. O. M. Melsness, Director of Child Welfare, at the above address and he will request a copy from the appropriate court.

2. British Columbia

The Ministry of Human Resources gives all non-identifying information available to an adopted adult who enquires in writing. There is a written policy and procedures manual on this for social work staff, which is being revised to more fully state the policy. Expect to wait longer than a month to receive non-identifying background information, although the department hopes to speed up the service.

Identifying information is never given out. The Ministry of Human Resources does not give copies of adoption orders to adopted adults, but a statement confirming that there is a record of adoption, which does not reveal original identity, can be obtained on written request.

No change in policy is contemplated. However, all policies and procedures relating to adoption are currently under review in relation to, among other things, their relevance to current adoption issues. Direct enquiries to:

Family and Children's Services, Adoptions
Ministry of Human Resources
614 Humboldt Street
Victoria, British Columbia
V8W 3A2

3. Manitoba

All non-identifying background information is available on written request from the provincial adoption services office and the wait is one month or longer. No identifying information is given out except with the consent of all the persons involved. Copies of adoption orders are available to adopted adults on formal application to and at the discretion of the county court that granted the adoption. One copy of the order is given to the adoptive parents at the time of adoption.

The provincial adoption office will not facilitate reunion unless it is known that all parties consent. "There is no machinery or programme to enable us to search for birth parents or adopted persons," said Miss Ruth C. Raven, Programme Executive, Adoptions, Child and Family Services. A change in policy regarding release of information and reunion is under consideration in Manitoba. Direct enquiries to:

Programme Executive, Adoptions
Child and Family Services
Manitoba Department of Health and Social Development
Community Services Division
831 Portage Avenue
Winnipeg, Manitoba
R3G 0N6

4. New Brunswick

Until recently, non-identifying background information was available to adopted adults from the Department of Social Services in New Brunswick.

As of November 1, 1978, a new policy regarding disclosure of information in closed adoption records has been in effect. Information now is available only from the Minister of Justice, who must give permission for access to closed adoption files. Information is given, by the Minister's decision, only for —

(a) legitimate reasons of health,

(b) administration of an estate,

(c) reasons relating to law enforcement, or

(d) reasons relating to the solemnization of marriage.

"Since such information would be limited to factual data with no necessity for interpretation or counselling, our department has taken the position that all requests should be handled by the Department of Justice," reported Ann Bell, Adoption Coordinator, Department of Social Services.

If you wish to apply for information or to comment on this change in policy, write to:

Minister of Justice
Department of Justice
P.O. Box 6000
Fredericton, New Brunswick
E3B 5H1

5. Newfoundland and Labrador

All non-identifying background information is available to adopted adults in writing on request from the Department of Social Services, within a month. Identifying information is never released. Copies of adoption orders are available on request from the Director of Child Welfare. The department does not facilitate reunions. Social workers do have written policy of procedures regarding the information that can be released. Direct enquiries to:

Director of Child Welfare
Department of Social Services
Government of Newfoundland and Labrador
Box 4750
St. John's, Newfoundland
A1C 5T7

6. Northwest Territories

Adult adoptees may obtain non-identifying background information and copies of adoption orders on written request. Be prepared to wait longer than one month for this information. No identifying information is available from the Northwest Territories.

Few requests for information have been received to date about the approximately 2 000 adoptions that have been completed in the Northwest Territories. There have been no requests for reunion and no counselling is provided regarding disclosure of information or reunion. Direct enquiries to:

Superintendent of Child Welfare
Department of Social Services
P.O. Box 1320
Yellowknife, Northwest Territories
X1A 2L9

7. Nova Scotia

Non-identifying information is available in Nova Scotia, but frequently there is little information on file. The information can be obtained from the provincial office of the Department of Social Services; the time involved depends on the availability of information and what is being requested.

Identifying information is available occasionally when the adopted person has reached the age of majority and when there is mutual agreement or consent between the adopted person and the birth parents, and when there is reasonable assurance that the giving of the information will not be detrimental to one or more of the parties. The department had facilitated in arranging 12 reunions as of August 1978, according to the above terms.

Copies of adoption orders are not given out, but a certificate of adoption may be given with the following particulars of the adoption:

(a) The name, after adoption, of the person adopted and, if known, his or her date of birth and birth registration number

(b) The names of the adoptive parents

(c) The name of the court granting the order for adoption and the date of the order

Each social worker has been provided with policy and procedure for maintaining data for the sealed adoption record. The policy on adoption enquiries is circulated to each agency and is available to every worker who is interested or who has obligations with respect to it.

There may be some minor adjustments to the existing policy in Nova Scotia but the main elements will probably remain unchanged for some time to come, according to Kevin Burns, Director, Family and Children's Services, Department of Social Services. Direct enquiries to:

Director, Family and Children's Services
Department of Social Services
P.O. Box 696
Halifax, Nova Scotia
B3J 2T7

8. Ontario

Legislation for a three-party reunion registry has been passed by the Ontario legislature and, at this writing, was expected to be in operation by the spring of 1979. This is a voluntary disclosure of information registry, with counselling provided for all parties involved. Birth parents and birth "children" (the adopted person) will be able to independently ask to be included in the registry and when names match up, disclosure of information will be possible providing the adopting parents give their consent.

Guidelines for operation of the registry had not been written when this information was obtained, but the expectation was that some accommodation would be made for dealing with cases where the adopting parent(s) is elderly or infirm.

Non-identifying background information is available to adopted adults, on written request, from the agency that arranged the adoption, and usually can be obtained in two weeks. Aside from the new registry, identifying information is not available except, usually, for reasons of health. A social worker acts for the adopted person in contacting the birth parent.

Copies of adoption orders are available sometimes from the Director of Child Welfare or the court. Policy and procedures for disclosure of information are included in the Child Welfare Act.

Direct enquiries for non-identifying background information to the appropriate Children's Aid Society in Ontario.

To apply for a copy of the adoption order or to add your name to the new disclosure registry, contact:

Director of Child Welfare
Ministry of Community and Social Services
Queen's Park
Toronto, Ontario
M7A 1E9

9. Prince Edward Island

Non-identifying background information is available on written request from the Department of Social Services in Prince Edward Island. Be prepared to wait longer than a month for the information. Identifying information is available only by court order of the Supreme Court of Prince Edward Island. A copy of the adoption order, which does not contain identifying information is given to the adopting parents at the time the order is made. The file is then closed and further copies may be obtained only through the court.

New child welfare legislation prepared for 1979 provides for the reunion of adoptees with original parents, after the adoptee reaches the age of 18, on the mutual consent of both parties. The proposed legislation had not been enacted at this writing. "It could be modified or set aside," reported James B. Mair, Coordinator, Children in Care, Department of Social Services. "We are hopeful the new legislation will more than adequately meet the need for disclosure and reunions." For information write to:

Adoption Coordinator
Children in Care
Department of Social Services
P.O. Box 2000
Charlottetown, Prince Edward Island
C1A 7N8

10. Quebec

Write to the agency that arranged your placement for all non-identifying background information, which takes about a month in Quebec. A court order is required for identifying information. This is sometimes available if the natural parent and the adoptee have shown interest in obtaining means to meet each other.

"There might be other reasons that the court may consider, but right now I don't know of any," said Monique Perron, Bureau d'adoption du Quebec. Copies of adoption orders are not available to adopted adults but a certificate of the adoption order is available to the adopted adult or to the adoptive parents. The reason for this is that the order contains identifying information.

The department does not facilitate reunions. A White Paper of November, 1976 foresees a change in policy regarding the release of information and reunion, and new legislation is anticipated. Direct enquiries to:

Monique Perron
Bureau d'adoption du Quebec
Ministere des Affaires Sociales
Gouvernement du Quebec
Quebec City, Quebec

11. Saskatchewan

All non-identifying background information is available on written request from the provincial adoption office. It takes two weeks to a month to obtain this information. Identifying information sometimes is available, providing both the adoptee and natural parent(s) request contact.

Copies of adoption orders are available to the adoptee on written request. This department has made ten to fifteen reunions possible in the past two years, when requested by both parties, according to Gerry Jacob, Director, Resources for the Adoption of Children Program. The policy followed in Saskatchewan is under review. Direct enquiries to:

Adoption Coordinator
Department of Social Services
1920 Broad Street
Regina, Saskatchewan
S4P 3V6

12. Yukon Territory

Only non-identifying background information is available from Yukon Territory on written request, but a copy of the adoption order might be obtained if there is no identifying information on it. It varies, depending on the time of adoption. In special circumstances identifying information might be available.

Counselling would be provided along with disclosure of information and reunion planning "if it ever came up," according to Jim Davie, Director of Child Welfare. The Yukon Territory has completed 496 adoptions to date and has received only three requests for information about origins from adopted adults in the past two years. There are plans to review the Yukon's legislation on adoption within the next few years. New adopting parents are now being advised about changing adoption concepts and "we deal quite fully with the possibilities of search," Davie said.

Non-identifying background information usually can be obtained in two or three weeks. Direct enquiries to:

Director of Child Welfare
Department of Human Resources
P.O. Box 2703
Whitehorse, Yukon Territory
Y1A 2C6

APPENDIX 2

PRIVATE RESOURCES

a. ADOPTION ACTIVIST GROUPS

The following organizations and groups promote changes in adoption legislation and practice, and assist adopted adults, birth parents and adopting parents, former wards and others with the search and reunion process. The names and addresses listed are subject to change.

Adoptees in Search
Box 41016
Bethesda, Maryland 20014

Adoption Forum of Philadelphia
Box 5607
East Falls Station
Philadelphia, Pennsylvania 19129

Adoptees Liberty Movement Association (ALMA)
P.O. Box 154
Washington Bridge Station
New York, New York 10033

and

P.O. Box 112
Lomita, California

and

Mrs. Doreen Peacock
95 Rudston Avenue
Wolviston Court Estate
Billingham
Cleveland, England TS 22

Concerned United Birthparents, Inc.
P.O. Box 513
Northgate Station
Seattle, Washington 98125

Jigsaw International
39 Manifold Road
Blackett
Sydney, Australia

Orphan Voyage
Cedaridge, Colorado 81413

Outside In
1240 S.W. Salmon St.
Portland, Oregon 97205

Search
P.O. Box 1432
Litchfield, Arizona 85340

Soundex Reunion Register
P.O. Box 2312
Carson City, Nevada 87701

Triadoption League for Justice
P.O. Box 5218
Huntington Beach, California 92646

Truth Seekers in Adoption
P.O. Box 286
Rosco, Illinois

b. PARENT FINDERS GROUPS
1. Alberta
Mrs. Penny Callan
334 Millbourne Road East
Edmonton, Alberta
T6K 3B2

Mrs. Mandy Martin
P.O. Box 971
Okotoks, Alberta
T0L 1T0

Mrs. Sandra Pope
P.O. Box 125
Lougheed, Alberta
T0B 2V0

2. British Columbia
Parent Finders
P.O. Box 34402
Station D
2405 Pine Street
Vancouver, British Columbia
V6J 4P3

Mrs. Robyn Shaw
D-4 7155 E.T.C. Highway
Kamloops, British Columbia
V2C 4T1

Mrs. Julie McWilliams
7754 Lancaster Crescent
Prince George, British Columbia
V2N 3T6

Mrs. Barbara Trowsdale
4726 Elk Lake Drive
Victoria, British Columbia
V8Z 5M6

3. Manitoba
Mrs. Laurie Mason
361 Templeton Avenue
Winnipeg, Manitoba
R2V 1S6

4. New Brunswick

Mrs. Irene Praeg
P.O. Box 263
Rothesay, New Brunswick
E0G 2W0

5. Nova Scotia

Mrs. Audrey Close
95 Coronation Avenue
Halifax, Nova Scotia
B3N 2M7

6. Ontario

Parent Finders Inc.
28 York Valley Crescent
Willowdale, Ontario
M2P 1A7

Mrs. Virginia Mason
219 Ellington Drive
Scarborough, Ontario
M1R 3Y2

Mrs. Wendy Redmond
393 Upper Ottawa Street
Hamilton, Ontario
L8T 3S9

Mrs. Mary Beth Hoy
194 Monmore Road
London, Ontario
N6G 3A6

Mrs. Sharon Phillips
P.O. Box 13102
Kanata, Ontario
K2K 1X3

Mrs. Joanne Jeffrey
1357 Moy Ave.
Windsor, Ontario
N8X 4S5

Mrs. Marilyn Billone
R.R. 2
Kitchener, Ontario
N2G 3W5

Mrs. Sandra Pilon
Mill St.
Singhampton, Ontario
N0C 1M0

7. Quebec

Mr. Don McMahon
P.O. Box 441
Pointe Claire, Quebec
H9R 4G9

Mr. Claude Samuel
C.P. 144
Repentigny, Quebec
J6A 5H7

8. Saskatchewan

Mrs. Elaine Hartt
209 — 929 Northumberland Ave.
Saskatoon, Saskatchewan
S7L 3W7

Mrs. Heather Adam
P.O. Box 334
Simpson, Saskatchewan
S0G 4M0

9. United States — New York

Marie Pauline Lamarche
P.O. Box 737
Port Washington
Long Island, New York 11050

APPENDIX 3

OTHER RESOURCES

Registrar General
New Register House
Princes Street
Edinburgh, Scotland EH1 3YT

Registrar General
New Register Office
49 Chichester Street
Belfast BT1 4H1
Northern Ireland

Registrar General's Office
Custom House
Dublin
Republic of Ireland

Association of British Adoption and Fostering Agencies
4 Southampton Road
London, England WC1B 4AA

Registrar General
St. Catherine's House
10 Kingsway
London, England WC2B 6JP

The above address is the general register of births, deaths and marriages in England and Wales, in case you wish to apply for any of those documents during search. Adopted persons 18 and over who wish to apply for their original birth records should write to the above address for an application form and advice as to procedure. If you already know your original parent(s) name, include that information.

Public Record Office
Chancery Lane
London, England W.C.2

The Society of Genealogists
37 Harrington Gardens
London, England S.W. 7

The Society has Boyd's *Marriage Index* and more than 4 000
Parish Register transcripts.

The Librarian
National Library of Wales
Aberystwyth, Dyfed SY23 3BU

The Secretary
Scottish Genealogy Society
St. Andrews Society Rooms
24 Hill St. (Castle St. end)
Edinburgh, Scotland

General Reference & Bibliography Division
Library of Congress
Washington, D.C. 20540

Write to request *Guides to Genealogical Research — A Selected
List.* The library houses thousands of American and foreign
genealogies.

Ministry of Social Welfare
State of Israel
8 King David St.
Jerusalem, Israel

Genealogical Reference Desk
Public Archives of Canada
395 Wellington St.
Ottawa, Ontario
K1A 0N3

Saskatchewan Genealogical Society
P.O. Box 1894
Regina, Saskatchewan
S4P 3E1

Genealogical Society
Wolstraat 39
B - 2000
Antwerp, Belgium

The Family History Association of Canada
P.O. Box 69492
Vancouver, British Columbia
V5K 4W6

BIBLIOGRAPHY

Paton, Jean M. *The Adopted Break Silence: Forty Men and Women Describe Their Search for Natural Parents.* Philadelphia: Life History Study Centre, 1954.

Paton, Jean M. (Pseudonym of Ruthena Hill Kittson), *Orphan Voyage.* New York: Vantage Press, 1968.

Sorosky, Arthur D., Baran, Annette, and Pannor, Reuben. *The Adoption Triangle. The Effects of the Sealed Record on Adoptees, Birth Parents, and Adoptive Parents.* Garden City, N.Y.: Anchor Press/Doubleday, 1978.

Sutherland, Neil. *Children in English-Canadian Society: Framing the Twentieth-Century Consensus.* Toronto: University of Toronto Press, 1976.

Triseliotis, John. *In Search of Origins: The Experiences of Adopted People.* London: Routledge and Kegan Paul, 1973.

Pine, L. G. *The Genealogist's Encyclopedia.* New York: Weybright and Talley, Inc., 1969.

ORDER FORM

SELF-COUNSEL SERIES

NEW TITLES:

Changing Your Name in Canada	3.50
Becoming a Canadian	3.50
Insuring Business Risks	3.50
Life Insurance for Canadians	2.95
Federal Incorporation and Business Guide	9.95
Drinking and Driving	4.50
Collecting Debts Successfully	3.50
Trust and Trust Companies	3.95

NATIONAL TITLES:

Canadian Guide to Death & Dying	3.50
Civil Rights in Canada	2.50
Consumer Law in Canada	2.50
Credit Law and Bankruptcy Handbook	3.50
David Ingram's Guide to Income Tax in Canada	3.50
How to Immigrate into Canada	2.95
Mike Grenby's Guide to Fighting Inflation in Canada	2.95
Our Accountant's Guide for the Small Business	3.50
Patients' Rights	1.95
Pollution and the Law in Canada	2.50
Retirement Guide for Canadians	4.95
Starting a Successful Business in Canada	4.50
Successful Job-Hunting in Canada	1.95
Tax Savings Plans in Canada	3.95
Unemployment Insurance Handbook	2.95
What to Do When the Taxman Comes	2.95

PROVINCIAL TITLES:

Divorce Guide
☐B.C. 5.95   ☐Alberta 6.95   ☐Ontario 7.95

Employee/Employer Rights
☐B.C. 2.95   ☐Alberta 2.95   ☐Ontario 2.95

Marriage & Family Law
☐B.C. 3.95   ☐Alberta 3.95   ☐Ontario 3.95

Fight That Ticket
☐B.C. 3.50   ☐Alberta 1.95   ☐Ontario 2.50

Incorporation Guide
☐B.C. 9.95   ☐Alberta 9.95   ☐Ontario 9.95   ☐Man./Sask. 9.95

Landlord/Tenant Relations
☐B.C. 2.95   ☐Alberta 2.50   ☐Ontario 2.95

Real Estate Guide
☐B.C. 4.50   ☐Alberta 3.95   ☐Ontario 3.95

Small Claims Court Guide
☐B.C. 3.95   ☐Alberta 2.50   ☐Ontario 2.95

Probate Guide
☐B.C. 9.95   ☐Alberta 9.95   ☐Ontario 9.95

Wills/Probate Procedure
☐Sask./Man. 3.50

Wills
☐B.C. 3.95   ☐Alberta 3.50   ☐Ontario 3.50

PACKAGED FORMS:

Incorporation
☐B.C 7.95   ☐Alberta 6.95   ☐Ontario 8.50   ☐Man./Sask. 7.95

Divorce
☐B.C. 6.95   ☐Alberta 6.95   ☐Ontario 6.00

Probate
☐B.C. 8.95   ☐Alberta 7.95   ☐Ontario 10.00

Sell Your Own Home   3.95
Rental Agreement   3.50
Will & Estate Planning   3.95

Note: All prices subject to change without notice.

— —

Cheque or Money Order
(plus 5% sales tax where applicable) enclosed.

Name _____

Address _____

City _____

Province _____

Postal Code _____

If order is under $6.00, add 30¢ for postage and handling.

— —

Please send orders to:

INTERNATIONAL SELF-COUNSEL PRESS LTD.
306 West 25th Street
North Vancouver, British Columbia
V7N 2G1

NOTES

NOTES

NOTES